All in Animal Time

Karólína Rós Ólafsdóttir

SPAM Press
Glasgow 2023

Did you order this day from a brochure?
You are a hairy miracle and I have earth-
worms between my toes and there is
singing. There are small brown birds.
Wow! With caps! There is soft grass/
fleece/blanket breadsoft worm skin
your hair, it's just so good   !   to lay
in sun and not wonder where electricity
comes from or pus we are so lucky
to lie here just   and earthworms
cause time only counts when they
surface then it expires, earthworms
that always return in rain and sell me
this day from a green brochure, soft.

Prenatal Care

It's all about cupping your palms, pressing
the fingers together so there is no seeping
and just collect. Rain, dew, drool only
of friends and lovers, puddlewater, cola, dog
saliva, summer tears, dregs and any kind of spitting.
This is the correct soak, run with it, home, pruney fingers
every day you are closer to filling the tub to give birth
in the world be honest from the very start, it's best

In the swimming pool showers

We've left our shoes outside, socks off first on the white tiles
we undress in harmony. Look at us now, four generations in
our underwear. Turning the tap, everyone sees naked, breast,
stomachs showering, scriptures of blue stretch marks across
bellies reading devotion to these shapes. We are one; pussy,
big toe, body, scrubbing, rubbing our pubic hairs in sync, coming
clean together. Plush curves sway. Bending, borrowing shampoo.
This is wisdom. Loose hair and lint evaporates. Here, everything
is holy. Our knees even, the fingers find nooks: *skip no body part.*
One body reminds another to use soap, frothing white. Look at us
now, we are wet and one body for a moment. The shuffle of towels
divides us up again clean clean again we are us, not one big
anymore. Slowly leaving, it is again holy, to have borrowed
extra-volume shine conditioner from a stranger, tying your shoes
to then walk into the day smelling like her.

Automatic Speech Recognition

When you can hear the robins through the chimney
from the neighbour's garden, silence crawls
from under the glass, it lives, there, between stone
grey couches stretches its arms, its legs, jumps
to grandmother's lap and curls up on the beige
corduroy, happens suddenly, not a certain time
of day silence is one, increasingly challenging,
shouting silence and flat and cold and damp, it is
definitely damp, not to give in, grandmother rises,
silence falls on the parquet, grandmother walks
to the small black box by the radio and whispers
Alexa, Alexa, play classical guitar. The black box
starts with a Spanish ballad and it becomes invisible,
silence, grandmother takes off her slippers and stuffs
them in the chimney, just ballads not robins, has not
been barefoot in ages, has not been alone before, has
thousands and thousands of ballads in the little
black box *Alexa, Alexa, how is the weather in London?*
Alexa how is the weather in Skåne? Alexa, Alexa, whatever
happened to Monica Lewinsky and how many grams
in a cup, please, classical guitar please, always polite
to Alexa in case of silence is a teenager now, increasingly
challenging, shouting silence and flat and cold and moist,
it is definitely moist, not to give in, grandmother stops
wearing slippers, hears the skin on wood, claps!
Alexa, Alexa play Johnny Cash! and candles that smell

nice and silence is so heavy it crawls up the chest
presses the soft pale skin, varicose veins, liver-spots,
printed onto silence's neck *Alexa how many people live*
in the Congo all maps seem to have tripled in size
as silence glues them to the glass table, see all that sea,
silence points to grandmother puts the slippers on, sherry,
Alexa, Alexa how much does a whale weigh there is no
measurement for silence but humpbacks are thirty
thousand kilograms and it only takes five hundred grams
to make rye, flour, the house – *Alexa what is the history*
of bread – gets smaller, just in case silence is all grown,
increasing at night, spreading silence and round and cold
and soaking wet, it is definitely soaking her feet in the wash
-tub grandmother, slippers off again, not to give in, moves
the crooked toe, small circle, writes cursive 'buy marzipan'
remembers this is everyone's washtub, warm and mint green,
Alexa, Alexa play classical guitar and tell me the story
of the thieves in the night and the child and the tree and
please whatever happened again to Monica Lewinsky

Wading the Creek

I remember silky mud like this one
time before, fishing probably. I remember bright green algae,

just in, the guide explained. I remember drawing
my stick through it and it splitting like grass would but falling

together again. I remember falling together again
the current pulling the waders to 'be quiet by the swans'

to be knee-deep in clay-sewer-eel-crab-home, enjoy it.
I remember seeing this tire so many times before

thinking of all the ways it could have arrived shored up
by the sediment, all the ways I could have arrived

differently, I remember dead crabs with beehive
bellies, shells in the black sand (back home) while these,
                                                    crawling,

I remember wanting to go down here, so many times
I remember various reasons. The guide speaks about

the spring tide, referring to 'jump 'not 'season'.

How to spell spring

A horse is a type of dog
and fish in the sea are happy
it is sunny (finally!) and I am
being told this by a five-year-old
with remarkable spelling abilities
and I agree that 'soshage' should
be spelled like that. We are sitting
on the front step when spring arrives
pot-bellied, in goosebumps, khaki
shorts of course and a tuxedo
t-shirt, it stops briefly to shout
at the parakeets feasting on cherry
blossom flowers, leaves as quickly
into an electronic garage I ask
'is a bicycle a type of dog too?'
'Don't be silly' says the five year old
and throws his orange peel towards
the birds – 'bicycles can't breath'.

Formaldehyde

I didn't have any syrup and now we have forever-peaches

so we don't need to store the jar in a dry dark place, like potatoes
or our ghosts. I will try sell it at the local-weekend-corner-
market for *endlessness* or *eternity*, whoever bids best,
yes! I will have an auction! 'Peaches, peaches a jaaaar
full of forever-peaches! Peaches, peaches…' speak as fast
as I can or exchange them for a shiny little
bug, something that flies (but not too fast) and shimmers
in sun (but not too bright) and lives for longer
than the average bug, or rather, since bug life expectancy
is not great right now, I will sell them online, for a kilo
of Camel Hair, next day delivery, I will make a rug,
for a wall, checkered, or with eyes, sell that too and get a box
of used taxidermy tools, in good condition, and then we,
and the bugs, can be forever too, like the peaches,
in the sun, the thick   liquid,   shimmer.

sonnet;

and that's what's it like living
in a lighthouse; snowblind and crashing
on the shore; I have heard frog legs dance under salt; I hear
drilling through all windows; snails making love for 2 to 12
hours; fermented dairy always lasts longer than labelled;
the cat looses that bet and gets a tattoo of my neighbours'
cockatoo; counting fourteen coins repeatedly just to make
sure; it sounds like all fish are deaf according to this; I've
only been mistaken for a devil underwater; sometimes a
face just looks like a wet woollen hat; Mondays are pretty
quiet there; today, not as expected, it is rather orange;
kicking is my medicine of choice; however, the problem is
underground and you are not authorised to go underground.

Lunch break duty

All the children are slapping each other on the playground today
like it's the new big thing. I'm devastated and chilly, the sun tricked
us it was spring again, window weather. The world pretends
to be sweet all the time

                              trying to focus on knitting a star-pattern
mitten I see a light grey moth heading for the wool of green and
cream I raise my palm, open, flat

                                  the sound of skin on skin
softened, finally, thank god it's getting colder. How is it soft
and stretched like a drum?

                         How is an elephant
slide a battlefield? I get sadder every day, standing in my lanyard.
Wishing I could cushion everything. Hands, cheeks, ground,
everywhere they are playing sometimes soft but too often heavy
beats, hands, boom, beat.

my algorithm says

search 'eyeshadow tutorial'
search 'pantry organisation'
search 'new cat memory'
search 'vaporwave aesthetic'
search 'dance photography'
search 'climbing a tree'
search 'bisexual relationship quotes'
search 'raccoon riding crocodile'
search 'teacher outfit'
search 'farmhouse girl decor'
search 'cyborg fruit mix'
search 'delicate tattoo'
search 'how to peace
        summer self development crochet bikini analog
terrarium 90's sneaker adventure this is what i want you
to see'

*

We have discovered a black hole
on our doorstep.

It is starving and that's what makes it so dark

apparently

we don't know what black holes like
to eat other than stars and interstellar gas
and we are currently on a budget; tuna in cans your step
mothers' lentil soup my bag of dried fish since I last went home.
2kg popcorn for 3.99.

It is much easier with dogs and humans
everyone likes buttered toast and pasta with nothing
            on it.

You read   *How to care for a place where gravity pulls too hard?*

*How to keep your matter (that is squeezed into a tiny place)
happy and healthy?*

and I arrange shells around its edges like one does
to mark the flowerbed from the weeds.

We measure thousand light years
in fly lives and convert that to human
lives through macaroni diagrams to try understand
and see how long we have

to learn how to feed enormous or supermassive
unexpected voids

in space.

(sonnet)

I have lost (or maybe misplaced? (I might find it
(tonight?) again (unlikely))) **the boat** (it was a rowing boat
(blue) that belonged to my grandfather (Jon (mothers' side))
he gave it to me (birthday present (25 years old)) after injuring
(falling (football with grandkids)) his shoulder (left) and couldn't
fish (also retired)) **to this anchor** (covered in barnacles).

106.500.000 km² Grand Drape

The Atlantic Ocean is the curtain of this new three part theatre
piece that relies heavily on seventeen large oboes that never play
all at once and never when the lights are on. The backdrop is
an impressionist oil painting of a storm, blue strokes still drying.

For the plot to function I have to stay on stage the whole scene
with the flamethrower and the old lady pressing flowers
in-between pages of a travel guide from April last year.

> As long as I am in London you could be alive in Berlin.
> As long as the moss green Thames rises and falls in my
> lower eyelid you could be having toast with butter and
> Aromat only.

In the second half I am dressed like a Victorian maid with a
dolphin butler who never faces the audience. I know you would laugh
about it, draw a caricature on a small institutional napkin.

The only real critique we got in the paper was that they didn't like
that the grand drape never lifts but they don't understand

we would all drown if it did so.

for Margeir

Your mother is making us trout for dinner.

The bottom of the sea has many things in common with your
parent's basement. When you look down it is dark and damp

and you can't really recall what anyone put down there. In the sea
of your parent's basement I find a photo of my skull, scattered

arrows, two mammals we never managed to meet, the first fish
that crawled up a sandy shore. The arrows point and explain: fish

skull, my skull, three red marks. Hammer, anvil, stirrup, originally
in their possession. And there, we kind of look alike. Large head,

slim nose, wide open eyeholes. We claim too much too quick
too often. There are so many things we cannot do like. Flying

without licenses and life jackets, growing great long teeth. Never
going to the dentist. The three small bones in our ears were first

theirs. For chewing the smallest swimming flea, shrimp cocktails.
For grinning out of the corner of their mouths. For cursing.

Licking. Kissing. Like the fish migrated, these bones crawled from
linking jaw to skull, headed inwards. These three small bones

now for us: hearing ABBA from the apartment below us, the cat
when it's stuck in a closet, flatmate having loud (good) (bad) sex,

sirens, good news we then forget. We can thank fish for that
to start with. I'm not sure they have settled there, our ear

bones might come out of the darkness to find a new place
on our face. Like the fish from the sea from your parent's

basement found new places in dry holes, sand, the velvet arm
-chair in the living room. Since we now know that the fish is

my great greatest grandmother, we should send it cards more,
call more often. Your mother has set the table. Butter, salt,

potatoes we are sitting with this knowledge gaping like the live
poached trout that in his first encounter with the burning

water turns cyan blue, jerks his head back. Now seasoned with dill
we get more butter, spreading it gently on the still scales deciding

to be grateful we still strut around in circles, sprinkle salt, drown
out the noise, pop on the radio, forget we boiled the pot initially.

And it might happen again tomorrow

Neither too soft nor too hard but all pale orange I am, again,
seeking to drive my hand through the day. Holding one end
(dawn) twisted around three fingers while extending myself
to the other (dusk). I am at the table a big woman, in flat knee
high boots for stability. For ground control. For this butter knife
yellow embroidered ducks in a line, edging the hem of the table
cloth. Surprise! I say, this is just for you, this circle of ducklings,
day. Aren't you happy to see me? All dressed up. The hairs on
thighs rising as I wait for day to open its mouth. It doesn't. Now
I start *open your heart to me baby* singing *I'll give you love if*
someone is surprised I haven't started yet. Done anything *nothing*
can stop me from trying I sing (explain). Still trying it is not
my fault you know, just like it said in that story, I shout (explain)
as the someone is going out wearing their small grey shoes routine
"it's allowed to resist, so it's resisting" while other days keep at it
in a gym, an office, bakery, I am alone with day and its slippery eel
time. I continue: one arm still extended, one glowing. I've given
each limb a permission to try enter the day. Of their own accord.
One tries force, butterknife, one tickling, stroking with a feather,
ostrich, one singing *open your heart with the key* one *one is such*
a lonely number one *ah, ah, ah.* It doesn't. Haven't you had this
happen? Standing up repeatedly. Milk gone. Blistering on the same
toe. Watching out, *(watch out, watch out).* Trusting *(watch out,*
watch out). Trying again. Finding new bread shrunken into a very
small loaf. Some days are just like that. Seeds suffering spring frost.

We each have our devil to drag
(*Icelandic saying*)

The devil I drag is wearing 'lemon-twist'
coloured roller skates and would have
a matching scrunchie if he had any hair.
The string between my shoulders and his
uncut mahogany claw is long, I rarely see
the end he plays with. When the string
shrinks he does not crawl up on my shoulders
to weigh me down or breathe cruel thoughts
down my running shirt. He glides along
in the park, playfully, so people think we like
each other and as I start enjoying the crunch
of soft gravel he lists all the names I don't want
to hear and maps the places we will not go visit.
The Devil's name is Josephine, today he wore
my windbreaker.

Flotsam

I woke on the back of one of those inflatable crocodiles.
It smelled of chlorine and rubber and smiled constantly
at the floating dock we were moving away from
with the steady breeze willows waltz to. We both looked
pale green, I from seasickness and the laser like sun-rays
(we were not in a pool). He, because rubber fades.
I did not have any shoes on but had my purple purse
with my sewing kit and a pamphlet from a beach cleaning.
'Paddle' he suddenly shouted and I plunged my hands
into the murk. 'To shore' he added 'quick!' His urgency
scared me and I looked around for sharp debris,
submarines. I did not know his name yet. 'What
is going on?' I asked and he replied 'I'm in love
and I have to tell her' 'Who are you in love with?'
'The pier! Paddle!' the crocodile cried through
a printed row of cream canine teeth. Ah, I thought,
obviously, and as my kelp tangled fingers paddled on
I fell in love with the crocodile, the light squeaking
of the rubber and the green. As we got closer I knew
there would be a duel and the only way to prevent it
was to reach for a needle, now, and the one I picked happened
to have the last of a twine in its eye, a thin pale, pale green twine.

Survey

Who else has this dagger
through their skull, right
above the right eye?

Head full of pissing
ants, just small fires
and fears. Asking

for ketchup afraid
it's asking too much.
Who else finds your face

in the smaller half of a fig
and now cannot eat it.
Just images - roadkill

hedgehogs, the various
shapes of wounds, foliage,
vibrator, blue, smiley face,
needle in my eye, who else.

Dear _____, you bastard

never showing you pale
little face up dark deep
eyes where have you been
all summer around the
world and not one lousy
postcard touring Europe.
I seem to never catch
you at the right time
I imagine: mid-stage, mid
line about the metal hand,
mid Latvian airport security
mid stubbing your small
big toe and you called back
midday I at work teaching
ten-year-olds to pronounce
pebb-els, pebb-els, and one
time eating at my aunt's
house, again, one time during
math, one times one times
one we seem to have made
this a habit, multiply, I saw you
were here while I was –
you jerk you didn't call me up
I repeat after Bernadette thinking
of your lazy eye, soft soft brown
always shoes without laces
and you don't text me till winter
and now I have left the place
we shared, dear, pale, call me
up afternoon sometime, I'll
try too, maybe dusk, in time,
maybe just after this.

A Crash Course in Volcanic

Say you come here for the smell of pine
and then it's sulphur and soot covered.
The ground surface is pushed up. Say
everyone has told you that this blue is
more blue. *The chamber inflates.* Say
you brought the whole of you. *The ground
surface subsides.* Say you feel the distance
pressure builds of the heart. *It opens.* Say
you see the red and luminous turning
grey as it meets the air. *Cascades in a fluid
state.* Say the thick flow is crusting your body
purple and thistly, all cavities are now young
rocks *bracketed by quiet intervals* and this
is a demonstration of something being one
hour old and simultaneously ancient and
solidified you can't count the days *for a flow
this thick to harden* say you wait it out
the magma chamber deflates say this is now
whole, of you. Stiff legged and crusted,
say you try, see how it goes. *Pressure builds.*

Lunch break duty II

Nancy's teaching everyone
how to make supper
for worms. The other
children move mud like
she does, wrap leaf tacos
with rocks their tiny
fingers like worms *for*
worms! they chant. Billy
kicks gravel at the feast
before line up shouting
"they don't need SUPPER!"
Someone is about to cry
another moved on already
by the swings, Nancy pulls
the pink jacket hood up,
her small head disappears,
in the polyester cave she
sniffles *for worms* yes I say
worms do yes darling,
her tiny fingers let go
of remaining leaves
the worms in tears
we watch them fall,
quietly, as everyone does.

my algorithm asks

how to control margins in a page document
how long is john wick 4
how is the paris agreement going this week
how to screenshot on pc
how many mannequins are there in the world
how to nutrition
how does it work to renew my old passport
how to screenshot on mac
how was the moon on my last last birthday
how wide is a queen's bed
how to write an essay about three women
how do i even know words
how to love lil wayne lyrics again
    yourself get rid of a cold fast trick chatbot drive a motorbike
to get you to come back after this is what i want you to learn

I used to cook a lot of lamb

stuffed baby thighs with garlic rubbed
rosemary, if oil companies were kinder
I would find it easier to quit – I would
know that in the future I'd manage to meet
the Lord Howe Stick Insect, have coffee
as glistening, slick, as its oblong body,
I would buy a brittle biscotti, to share,
he would say 'Darling, call me
Tree Lobster', I would blush, of course.

Twelve years later we are making house,
happy, out of gingerbread, we have
exterminated pesticide, paid our student
loans, making homemade pastry, rub his
back, gently, he says, 'Love, hand
me the oven mittens' I say 'Jim,
let me, I've got thumbs', the scent of spices–

Now, I eat hard tea crackers on the kitchen
floor, waiting for my 'two for one pound fifty'
in the oven. I see the sun steering clear
of windows. A man making everything
astroturf. Soil traumatised. Staring into
the yellow bulb above the tray I wish I was
too, built to withstand extreme temperatures.

sonnet?

Maybe I'll get it right this time.
                              Counting the moles
on your back or the shoulders? How many are there
usually? Of anything? They spell things out to you?
Can you read them in the mirror? They don't spell
but whisper? Is anything normal inside a room
after this long? Why I left that single hair in my arm-
pit? Are there always reasons for small communities?
Is this not your mouse? Is it paying rent? Do these
small stilettos belong to it? Oh, so these are my shoes
and my mouse and my rent? How many?

some days i open the google
maps map see the blue dot
pinging to feel grounded i watch
myself walk down the road past
the Birds Nest towards the creek
watch the blue circle slither on past
shops past buses pulsating down grey
lines, there i am, stop in a triangle of green

this is a portrait of me in nature

my body on this pale green shape
7:28, SE8 4RL, four-star review sycamore;
a common urban bastard

Landscape Painting Priorities

Paint a white sky, it is winter. Paint a sheep
lying on its side, yellow tilting head, bloating.
Paint twigs everywhere as there are no birds
left to make them nests. Paint pneumonia,
or listeriosis. Paint the six thousand wings
reported on the last hunting card. Registered
incidents only those in frame. Paint no more
growth. Paint it any time of day. Paint off-
road tire tracks, paint dross, any size suitable.

Put red smudges in the sky on the painting (one for each raven).

Drop by

I finally came to visit. All your neighbours
moss grown names local and green-hued
woman filling a bucket close by the water
even whispers here I hear each rock rub
against the other in the gravel under my shoe
only small things seem to move like stones like
old women's feet like fishflies like the ring of the car
keys in my pocket moving from one finger to the other
like I must say it doesn't suit you living like this and so I find
myself trying to enliven your lane humming Wu-Tang
in the cemetery like hey, you know, everybody's talking about
the good old days, right? Everybody! The good old days

well let's talk about the good old days

This is returning

There is an ad outside, massive, *Mallorca*
is calling. I am blanketed in snow once again

and not even home yet. The palm trees flicker
green and stringy every blast wind slap

in the face this is the coldest January this
century you're welcome static electricity beach

girl really enjoy this one, and that on a Monday
why do we stay in a place this frost-coated

I ask my mother who is not bothered by the sixth
storm this season have an apple now, she cuts

the round fruit to boats. This is how we've always
been feeling the sweet red crunch with our eyes closed.

sonnet &

twenty aircrafts
& it's not just Isaac
   that is crying
& boink
& chickens just
   everywhere
& sigh, pre-historic
   fuckers
& I am busy in this
   seven-day-salt-brine
& have no shoes
& there is no more room
   on the wall for neon
   green gravestones
& it is not soup
   weather yet
& it needs to starts
   with a car chase
& the chickens win
& we are happy for them
& fair enough
& if anyone can contain
   a world like
   an egg does
& if all they need is
   twenty aircrafts now

I have no objection

Get a Life: Ultimate Edition

Sul sul! It is great here! You have
made the right decision open
forehead glitch aside just a bug
in the system green hill Veronaville,
we have built house now pressed
'grow-up' self-interaction, have
the expansion pack *Apartment Life*
short hair, we are filling aspiration
bar hobby, woohoo, Baked Alaska
depending on the time of day. Seldom
oh feebee lay these days though not
many simoleons and ctrl+shift+c
<bugjartimedeacay off> does not
work in real life. We luv sugnorg.
I just wanted to let you know.
Head outside now. Dag dag. Enjoy.

Girl and a Friend

We are both youngest and most beautiful in here
whispered the girl to her friend. Even though we are
standing here in the shadow, neither bathing in the blue
bar light or the yellow one that is aimed at the band
added the other. Those Americans definitely want us
said the girl. Ye, definitely said the friend. Fuck, they
are lame said the friend in direct continuation. Yes,
I talked to one of them earlier, he was stupid anyway
answered the girl. Ha! That doesn't surprise me said
the friend and asked what did he say so stupid? He was
saying that there was so much cocaine in Iceland
because it would be easy to hide it in the snow the girl
explained. Jesus, sighed the friend. But he was at least
polite the girl shot in, said good evening. Well, that doesn't
really matter if you are just stupid said the friend. Yes,
maybe said the girl. We are at least both youngest
and most beautiful here repeated the friend.

Friend and a Girl

We have both been here longest and most often
whispered her friend to the girl. Even though we
feel it go by faster here, neither bathing in the green
December light or the yellow one beaming from
the lamppost added the other. Those days are definitely
getting us said the friend. Ye, definitely said the girl.
Fuck, this is hard said the girl in direct continuation.
Yes, I walked some earlier, it was stupid anyway
answered the friend. Ha! That doesn't surprise me said
the girl and added, where did you try go? Just as many
paces from the house as these legs allowed me explained
the friend pointing to the green, the curved knee,
crooked toe. Jesus, sighed the girl. It was at least outside
you know the friend shot in, you should try it. Well, that
doesn't really matter if you are just imaginary said
the girl. Yes, maybe said the friend. I have at least both been
here the longest and am the most…ended the girl.

<WE KNOW GIRLS IRL>

pink fleshed and all these

stickers on apples, wormy

hermit girls, laced boots up

Nicki Minaj's style, wtf as in

whispering to foxes (again)

running hands through green

buzzcut like its spring grass

girl scented purple and thistly

just as the inside of a rock is

something you can't hold in

the palm of your hand try

again cinnamon wrapped

mummy girl forever precious

object girl lasts so long piece

of flint around your neck in

leather string kind of type

we know the way it's written

in cursive *girl* mom with girl

babygirl drawing round heads

pigtails triangle bodies growing

up heartbreak girl waterproof

mascara expert that's the way

it's done around these parts

of them all over the cloud

shaped blanket knitted poly-

ester we know each thread

three-day loan at the library

girl written by another

girl moss growing that soft

space of no thanks and then

some more of that good

getting stuck in a hedge girl

in the rough large purple

knees and hips always walking

into corners some of it is

what we wanted and the other

sorted by freshness

the shoes you gave me are still on fire
my shorter arm has three blisters now

one is super shiny
one is firm
one yellow and wet and deflated

you'd never know that I'd tried to put them on
I have always collected small domes to protect
damaged surfaces, look at this one and this

one is luminous
one is marked with a sign: *Do not touch it, above all,*
                                    do not touch it

Wait for the sediment to settle

I serve everyone fruit from this cup.
Then coffee and after, lift the cup above
your head, three circles clock-wise and then
against, gathering your thoughts, blow a cross
inside it against the bad stuff, place it securely
on the nearest radiator. Lean it on a little plate.
Then you can see what awaits after this melon,
grains align, I read future from the lip: a hand
with four fingers, awkward incident, a number,
seven with five zeroes or a seven and dark dots
that bring sorrow; that if anything reminds you
of a foetus it probably is. Along the body:
the porcelain has pushed you soft lines: long
mail or! surprise! It's a long boat with coal or
sugar cubes in the foot you have circled me a past,
the letter L, you recognise it, a pigeon with a single
grape and a pair of dried feet in 39, prints, nothing
you don't know it lasts for a month, each cup's telling,
the blue gulls on the outside and if it wasn't
for standardised room sizes the length of my arm
I could serve everyone fruit from this cup and no suffer.

Back again again

That's her brother there and their father and that's his second
cousins cousins cat, don't you know anything anymore you have
not been keeping, clearly, up just like I am dating the first boy
you ever kissed now he has the same haircut, isn't that the cutest!
All the streets lead to other streets which lead to one big circle,
street, goes round everything no matter what direction: ocean
one side, land the other, cold ground between, hard, all around
us are my parents memories: they walked this hill, threw an egg
out the window of this school it is all marked long before my time
and I can make the rasp raven sound deep deep in my throat *all*
natur-al I joke meaning *me and that bird go way back* meaning
more to me than I expected. Driving the circle memories, stopping
briefly in the soft hollow surrounded by blueberries. Surrounded
by edges, waves erode making us both smaller, rounder, days
by years by years I make the rasp croak sound in my throat
while at it, being bird, an islander and a bird again, while at it.
I drive down a new road leading me to a new road to the shore,
circle, the very edge, here it is, of land, croaking.

sonnet!

Hands up! Millions of rats coming from the sewers! Rat, rat!
Another rat! They are all here with me! Robbing this bank!
Give us the stacks of coins you keep! We will use them to discover
elements in space! Local astronomers! Love! Sewers! I have given
up paying rent to someone that doesn't care about homes!
Bring us the coins, one for each feet, each hand, coin toes, knitting
hats for cold heads, cures, comets, go!

All in Animal Time

hands of a clock slow
clap for the common flea

images in cubic meters
fly across per second

my eyes do their best
to prevent children falling

glass breaking the way
a flower blooms but faster

can I love better through
a long-form article?

remembering while
post-it glue lasts

starfish notice the slowest
my pill daily a different delay

this video has been going
on for time unmeasured

writing this email feels
like milking a stone

I hope it finds you well
the slow anticipation

seeing someone write your name
the breaching of a whale watching

the pinwheel reveal you with a grey donkey
enlarged in fully rendered glory

What remains

I've sent a lot, left
red thread ends
to lead you out
of the heart (of
the maze), left
canopies because you
like the way leaves
shadow. What is
left is me and that
picture of a swan
which still doesn't
float and residue
of hands on page
ninety-eight, the trail
of your eyes on all my
poems, the swan card-
board cut-out sinks in the
fountain and everything
is still purple, no lilac
you would have said
but since you are not here,
it stays purple.

ACKNOWLEDGEMENTS

Thanks to the editors of *SPAMzine, magma poetry, daughterhood zine* and *Weavers magazine* where versions of some of these poems have previously appeared. Thank you Maria Sledmere and Mau Baiocco for your editorial advice, poetic insight and patience and for making this happen. Some of these poems were born in Sophie Robinson's and Rose Higham-Stainton's workshop *Devotion*, Maria Sledmere's workshop *Writing the Everyday* at Beyond Form Creative Writing, in workshops at Goldsmiths University with Jack Underwood and I am very grateful for the guidance and inspiration I found in those spaces. Thanks to my family and friends, my cats, my uncle's dog, my mother's old horse. Thank you Fred Turtle, Poppy Cockburn, Luke Mark and Sölvi Halldórsson for giving these poems headspace again and again. Thank you Boaz, Odda, Úlfur, Margrét, Lóa, Dana.

The sketch for 'Duck' (2021) is by Boaz Yosef Friedman, thank you for allowing me to include it, to use it for spying on animals pretending to be something else other than animals.

Cover design is taken from 'Untitled sketchbook page', gel ink on paper (2023) by Maura Sappilo.

not get raptured. This reasoning is part of the teaching some do to convince themselves that the rapture is occurring at a point that the scripture is not indicating. It is an example of the circular reasoning I addressed earlier. "This must be the rapture, because it is where it has to be if the rapture is pre-trib," they reason. I will address this further in the text when detailing the book of Revelation, including references to the church.

DEFINING THE PRE-TRIBULATION RAPTURE
(This is referring to the specific pre-Tribulation rapture teaching.)

Rapture

+ A coming of the Lord
+ Trumpet sound, particularly the last trump
+ Resurrection of the dead in Christ
+ Gathering together of the dead in Christ rising with those who are alive and remain to meet Christ in the air at Christ's coming. All are instantly changed in a twinkling of the eye from corruption to incorruption, mortality to immortality. (Resurrected body)

Pre-Tribulation Rapture

+ A coming of the Lord, just in the air to meet with those who have been raptured. Occurs before the seven-year Tribulation period and before the Antichrist is revealed.
+ Trumpet sound (not heard by anyone on the earth) May be symbolic.
+ The resurrection of the dead in Christ occurs.
+ There is a gathering together of the dead in Christ and those who are alive. All receive a resurrected body in a twinkling of an eye. Jesus takes all with Him back to heaven to await the end of the Great Tribulation. All will return with Jesus at His Second Coming to the battle of Armageddon and rule and reign with Him for a thousand years (Millennium.)

DEFINING THE POST-TRIBULATION RAPTURE

Rapture

- ✤ A coming of the Lord
- ✤ Trumpet sound, particularly the last trump
- ✤ Resurrection of the dead in Christ
- ✤ Gathering together of the dead in Christ rising with those who are alive and remain to meet Christ in the air at Christ's coming. All are instantly changed in a twinkling of the eye from corruption to incorruption, mortality to immortality. (Resurrected body)

Post-Tribulation Rapture

- ✤ The Second Coming of the Lord. Occurs at the last day of the Tribulation period at the coming of the Lord, not seven years earlier before the Tribulation period. What makes the coming of the Lord the last day of the Tribulation period, is that Jesus ends the battle of Armageddon and the time of tribulation. (It is interesting to note that Jesus said he would raise His own at the last day.)

John 6:40, 44b, 54

40 And this is the will of him that sent me, that every one which seeth the Son, and believeth on him, may have everlasting life: and I will raise him up *at the last day.*

44b and I will raise him up at the *last day.*

54 Whose eateth my flesh and drinketh my blood, hath eternal life: and I will raise him up at the *last day.*

- ✤ There is a trumpet sound. It is the last trump sound occurring at the seventh trump, the last of the seven trumpets that sound in the book of Revelation

✤ The resurrection of the dead in Christ occurs
✤ There is a gathering together of the dead in Christ and those that are alive.
   All receive a resurrected body in a twinkling of an eye.
   All meet Jesus in the air at His coming and go with Him to the battle of Armageddon.
   All rule and reign with Jesus for a thousand years (Millennium) after He ends the battle.

PRE-TRIB/POST-TRIB RAPTURE TABLE

Rapture: Coming of the Lord and gathering together of the body of Christ, including dead and living in new resurrected bodies.

Pre-Tribulation (Scriptures supporting a Pre-Trib rapture.)	Pending (Scriptures that need more verifying before placement.)	Post-tribulation (Scriptures supporting a Post-Trib rapture.)

This is a table we will fill out as we look at specific scriptures. When we read a scripture, we will ask the question, "Does this scripture fit the post-trib teaching? If it does, we will put that scripture under the post-trib column. Also, could the scripture align with the pre-trib teaching? If it doesn't fit one, then we will put it under pending. There may be something we have to establish from another scripture, and then we can move the scripture from the pending to where it fits. The scripture by itself may not fit one of the categories, but may later after we have looked at other scriptures.

We can now look at some specific scriptures and see where they fit on the table.

I Thessalonians 4: 13 – 18

13 But I would not have you to be ignorant, brethren, concerning them which are asleep, that ye sorrow not, even as others which have no hope.

14 For if we believe that Jesus died and rose again, even so *them also which sleep in Jesus will God bring with him.*

15 For this we say unto you by the word of the Lord, that we which are alive and remain unto the *coming of the Lord* shall not prevent them which are asleep.

16 For the Lord himself shall descend from heaven with a shout, with the voice of the archangel, and with the trump of God: and the dead in Christ shall rise first:

17 Then we which are alive and remain shall be *caught up together* with them in the clouds, to meet the Lord in the air: and so shall we ever be with the Lord.

18 Wherefore comfort one another with these words.

This is the first scripture that I discussed concerning the rapture. Read over this passage carefully. We will look at it in relationship to pre-trib or post-trib teaching. We know this is referring to the rapture—it is at the coming of Jesus, there is a trumpet, there is a gathering together. The dead in Christ rise first (This is referring to their bodies. The spirits of the dead in Christ are those whom Jesus brings with him when he comes,) and those who are alive and remain are caught up together to meet the Lord at His coming. Then we are with Him forever.

Does this fit the post-trib teaching? It is at a coming. We know His Second Coming is to the earth after the Tribulation period. There is a trumpet, a resurrection and gathering together. We meet Him in the air, and go with Him to the battle of Armageddon. He is coming and we meet Him. We will be with Him because we will rule and reign with Him for the thousand-year reign. So, yes, it supports the post-trib teaching.

The following is the way a person who believes in a pre-trib rapture will explain this scripture: This is not the coming of the Lord to the battle of Armageddon at the end of the Tribulation period when He comes to the earth. This time, he just comes into the air and we go up in the air to where He is. He then takes us back to heaven with Him. Then, seven years later, after the Tribulation period, when He actually comes to the earth, we come with Him.

Does this scripture, by itself, standing alone at this point fit the Pre-trib teaching? Does this scripture state that there is another coming before the Tribulation period? No. We will have to verify from other scriptures that there is a coming before the Tribulation or establish that the rapture is pre-trib. So far, we know about the post-trib coming of the Lord. This scripture, by itself, does not say there is another coming seven years earlier, before the Tribulation period.

I can give you a challenge as you read the scriptures. I challenge you to find another coming of the Lord. I will tell you this, having read the Word: You will not find another coming. The only thing that makes Jesus come at another time, besides at His Second Coming; the only thing that makes Him come only in the air seven years before His Second Coming is the pre-tribulation teaching. This scripture *is* the rapture and it tells us we will gather together to meet Jesus at His coming. The pre-trib doctrine requires another coming of Jesus, just in the air because the doctrine is saying the rapture is before the Tribulation period, not at the time of Jesus' Second Coming in which He ends the Tribulation period. Just to read this scripture by itself, and claim that Jesus only comes in the air, then comes to the earth later, cannot be done until you establish from other scriptures that the pre-trib doctrine is correct. This scripture does not tell us that.

Someone who has been taught a pre-trib rapture may ask, "Why would we go up in the air and turn around and come back to the earth? Because we are meeting Jesus at His coming. If it is Jesus who is coming, the question should be, "Why would He turn around and go back to heaven at His own coming? Who is doing the coming, and who is doing the meeting?

If you had a relative coming from Texas to stay with you at your house, and you are going to meet him at the airport; do you buy a ticket and go with him back to Texas? Or, would you and he go to your house? Jesus is coming, and we are meeting Him at His coming. This scripture is not saying that He is meeting us at our going to heaven, but that we are meeting Him at His coming. Do you see how a preconceived pre-trib teaching makes the scripture say something it isn't saying?

If the rapture is pre-trib than we have to make this scripture say that He is meeting us in the air to take us to heaven. The scripture says we are meeting Him at His coming. To where is Jesus coming?

We will need to strongly establish a pre-trib rapture before we can justify this as a pre-trib scripture.

We can put this in the post-trib column of the table. It will need to put it in the pending column for the pre-trib rapture until we can establish another coming or a pre-trib rapture.

Some other scriptures we can add to this are the ones concerning Jesus raising those who are His (those who are believers) at the *last* day. Everything changes when Jesus returns. There is an end to the Tribulation period and the battle of Armageddon. It is the last day before He sets up His rule and reign for a thousand years. (Scriptures for this will be discussed later.) These scriptures support a post-trib rapture, because before the tribulation (pre-trib) is years earlier and not the last day.

PRE-TRIB/POST-TRIB RAPTURE TABLE

Rapture: Coming of the Lord and gathering together of the body of Christ, including dead and living in new resurrected bodies.

Pre-Tribulation (Scriptures supporting a Pre-Trib rapture.)	Pending (Scriptures that need more verifying before placement.)	Post-tribulation (Scriptures supporting a Post-Trib rapture.)
	I Thes 4: 13 – 18 (Must establish another coming of the Lord or establish that the rapture is pre-trib.	I Thes 4:13 – 18
		John 6: 40, 44, 54

Notice on the table, that I have placed I Thessalonians 4:13 – 18 under Post-trib and under pending since we have to establish either a coming of the Lord or the pre-trib teaching before we can put it in the pre-trib column.

The next scripture passage I will discuss is 2 Thessalonians 2:1–12. This is from Paul's letter to the Thessalonians. This is one of those passages specifically in which some of the wording in the King James Version is not used the same today. There is nothing wrong with the wording, if you understand the old English terminology. In verse 7, the KJV uses the words 'let" and "letteth." Sometimes, if all you have is the KJV, you can look at other scriptures to understand a word. In Romans 1:13, Paul said he was going to come to the Romans, but he was "let." We can understand that this means he was hindered or held back. The New King James Version (NKJV) translates this word as "restrains." In verse 9, the KJV translation has the word after, not meaning coming next, but "like unto." The NKJV uses the wording "according to." I will refer to the NKJV for this passage.

2 Thessalonians 2:1 – 12 (NKJV)

The Great Apostasy

1   Now, brethren, concerning the coming of our Lord Jesus Christ and our gathering together to Him, we ask you,

2   not to be soon shaken in mind or troubled, either by spirit or by word or by letter, as if from us, as though the day of Christ had come.

3   Let no one deceive you by any means; for that day will not come unless the falling away comes first, and the man of sin is revealed, the son of perdition,

4   who opposes and exalts himself above all that is called God or that is worshiped, so that he sits as God in the temple of God, showing himself that he is God.

5   Do you not remember that when I was still with you I told you these things?

6   And now you know what is restraining, that he may be revealed in his own time.

7   For the mystery of lawlessness is already at work; only He who now restrains will do so until He is taken out of the way.

8   And then the lawless one will be revealed, whom the Lord will consume with the breath of His mouth and destroy with the brightness of His coming.

9   The coming of the lawless one is according to the working of Satan, with all power, signs, and lying wonders,

10   and with all unrighteous deception among those who perish, because they did not

receive the love of the truth, that they might be saved.

11 And for this reason God will send them strong delusion, that they should believe the lie,

12 that they all may be condemned who did not believe the truth but had pleasure in unrighteousness.

This passage is more or less the "holy grail," or it is the scripture that teachers of the pre-trib rapture use almost as the definitive case for support of the teaching that the rapture is before the Tribulation period.

The NKJV starts this passage with the phrase, "The great apostasy." This refers to a turning away from God, and the things of God and falling from the truth of God's Word.

Verses 1 – 2. Paul says, "concerning the coming of the Lord . . . and our gathering together to Him." What do you think this is talking about? (A coming of Jesus and a gathering together.) It is the rapture, isn't it? In verse 2, he is saying not to be troubled, thinking that this has already happened. Apparently, the Thessalonians had been sent a letter or told that this had already happened or was soon to happen, and Paul was reassuring them that, that wasn't the case.

Verse 3. Paul says not to let anyone deceive you. (We are often warned in end-time scripture not to be deceived.) He says "that day." What day? Paul says in verse 1 that the topic of discussion is the coming of the Lord and our gathering together unto him. That day will not occur until there is a falling away first and the man of sin is revealed. (The man of sin is referring to the Antichrist that comes during the Tribulation period.) Paul is saying that some things have to happen first, before the rapture will occur. Many have said that the apostles believed that Jesus could come back any minute. Paul didn't. He may have believed that Jesus would return in his day, but he obviously was explaining to the Thessalonians that some things had to happen that had not happened yet. As to the phrase "falling away," if you look it up in the Strong's Concordance, the Greek word is apostasia, meaning defection from the truth or a state of apostasy.

The church will become apostate. There are other New Testament scriptures to support this. Timothy 4:1 states that in the latter times some will give heed to seducing spirits and doctrines of devils. Paul said that people would have a form of godliness and deny the power (2 Tim. 3:5). There is going to be false doctrine that will come into the church, and people are going to receive it. In other words, there is going to be an apostasy. We are already seeing this beginning. Many churches today allow gay minister. (I am not judging a person who commits homosexual sin any more than I would be judging a person if I say a person living in adultery cannot minister (1 Cor. 6:9–11.) An adulterer or a bank robber is not insisting that their behavior not be called sin.) There are churches that read from the Quran, and they are accepting that Allah is the same God that we serve. (Jehovah God, the father of Jesus, is not Allah. Allah, if he isn't Satan, is a demon.) Some are teaching that there are many ways to heaven besides Jesus. This is not so.

John 14:6

6   Jesus saith unto him, I am the way, the truth, and the life: *no man cometh unto the Father, but by me.*

I was listening to an old interview from when George W. Bush was president in which he even said there is more than one way to heaven. He was asked specifically if the Muslims have the same God, and he said, "Yes, I believe they do." It is amazing how more and more apostate the church world (the major denominations) is becoming.

In verse 3 after the apostasy first, it then says in addition, the man of sin will be revealed. In other words, there will be an apostasy, and we will know who the Antichrist is before we get raptured. These two things at least will happen before we get raptured. Most pre-trib teachers teach that the man of sin (the Antichrist) will not, even cannot be revealed until the church is raptured. When you read this passage from verses 1–3, is this what it is saying? I read that the rapture will not take place until there is a falling away and the man of sin is revealed. Allow me to explain how this is framed by most pre-trib teachers. They take the phrase "falling away" and say someone has found some (obscure) translation somewhere that shows this could mean a "catching away." They grabbed hold of that and say that the rapture has to take place before the Antichrist can be revealed. This is rather a flimsy explanation for framing a major doctrine concerning the timing of the rapture. Yet if you have heard pre-trib teaching, you have heard this. But, again, that is not what this is saying. The falling away is not a catching away. You certainly do not see this translated this way in legitimate concordances such as Strong's. In addition, there is no other scripture that uses the term "falling away" to refer to the rapture. We have seen "caught up together" and "gathering together" but never falling away. Besides, it doesn't even fit in the scripture because Paul is saying that day (the coming of the Lord and our gathering together unto him) will not occur until there is a falling away first. Using pre-trib teachers' reasoning, Paul would be saying that the rapture cannot occur until the rapture occurs. This is an example of a preconceived idea creating circular reasoning. (The falling away means catching away, therefore the rapture has to take place before the Antichrist is revealed. Hence, the rapture has to occur before the Tribulation period.)

Verse 4. The man of sin will sit in the temple showing himself to be God. Some say that this may mean that there will be a temple built in Jerusalem. I have heard that this temple is ready to be built now. Even all the bowls and furniture are ready. It could be built in a matter of months. It could very well be the case that an actual temple will be built.

Before I address the "he who restrains" in verse 7, I want to point out the word, "breath," in verse 8. Paul is saying that Jesus will consume the Antichrist with the breath of his mouth and the brightness of his coming. The KJV says, "Spirit" of his mouth. The Greek word is pneumatic, and it does come from a word meaning breath. In medicine, from Latin, you can think of pneumonia (infection in the lungs), and pneumothorax, which means air in the thoracic (chest) cavity. However, this is the same word used throughout the New Testament for spirit and Spirit of God. Spirit is so much more than breath. This is why I like to use the KJV as a standard. Some words in newer translations just do not seem to go deep enough.

I Corinthians 2:10-11

10 But God hath *revealed* them unto us by his Spirit: for the Spirit searcheth all things, yea, the deep things of God.

11 For what man *knoweth* the things of a man, save the *spirit of man* which is in him? Even so the things of God knoweth no man, but the Spirit of God.

This passage shows that there is a spirit of man as well as a Spirit of God. We also can see that spirit knows. Breath does not know.

James 2:26 says that the body without the spirit is dead. There is a denomination that teaches that this just means breath, and that only our breath leaves our body when we die and returns to God. We just lie in the grave asleep until the resurrection. When we understand that spirit is more than breath, we realize that we are spirit beings, and it is "us" leaving our body, not just our breath. God is a Spirit. (John 4:24). He is not just a bag of air. We are spirit.

1 Thessalonians 5:23

23 And the very God of peace sanctify you wholly; and I pray God your whole spirit and soul and body be preserved blameless unto the coming of our Lord Jesus Christ.

Paul implies that to be absent from the body would be to be present with the Lord.

2 Corinthians 5: 6, 8-9

6 Therefore we are always confident, knowing that, whilst we are at home in the body, we are absent from the Lord:

8   We are confident, I say, and willing rather to be absent from the body, and to be present with the Lord.

Philippians 1:21, 23

21   For me to live is Christ, and to die is gain.

23   For I am in a strait betwixt two, having a desire to depart and to be with Christ; which is far better.

Just as Jesus spoke words to calm the storm (Matthew 4:39), He will use words (the spirit or sword of His mouth) to end the battle of Armageddon and destroy the Antichrist and his prophet.

Verse 6 says, "Now you know what is restraining that he may be revealed *in his own time*." As many times as I have read this scripture, it has just been very recently that I picked up on this phrase. Then, I heard a minister say it, which helped confirm my thought.[3] He will not be revealed until it is time. This may be the major reason for the restraint that has held the Antichrist from coming. It wasn't time in Paul's day, and it hasn't been time up to this point. Jesus' First Coming did not happen until it was time, and the Antichrist will not come until it is his time.

Galatians 4:4

4   But when the fullness of the time was come, God sent forth his Son.

Verse 7. He who restrains will restrain until he be taken out of the way. It also says that the mystery of iniquity (KJV) already works. I like this terminology better than the word lawlessness in the NKJV because lawlessness to me implies just the breaking of man's law. Iniquity is referring to God's law. (Although the Antichrist may do both.) Going sixty miles an hour in a thirty-mile speed zone is lawlessness, but it isn't necessarily iniquity. Perhaps it would be better to use this example: Having an abortion isn't breaking the law, but it is iniquity.

In Paul's day, there were those with an Antichrist (meaning against Christ) spirit.

There are a few ideas about what the "he who restrains" means. Some have said that the he is the church. The church has to be taken away by being raptured out before the Antichrist can come forth. It is the church that is restraining the Antichrist. As long as the church is in the world, he can't come. Others have said that the church has been referred to as "she" not "he" in the scriptures, so it is the Holy Ghost (Holy Spirit) in the church that restrains, and when the Holy Spirit goes out with the church, then the Antichrist can come forth. I have heard that the "he" is the hand of God, and when God removes His hand, the Antichrist can come forth.

I was reading this one day and meditating on it since I had heard all these ideas and just asked the question, "Who is he?" I am not saying this is revelation knowledge, and I could be wrong, but this is the answer I got. "Even He, the spirit of truth." This is from John 16:13 referring to the Holy Spirit. Okay, that is one of the ideas I had heard. Then I asked, "How is he taken out of the way?" This time, the answer was, "Read on." As I read on, I saw how that because people loved not the truth, they would believe a lie. Getting the answer to the question as the Spirit of Truth, referring to the Spirit of God helped me see this. The Holy Spirit is taken out of the way of a church when it becomes apostate and falls from truth. We have already been told there would be an apostasy. It is amazing how quickly denominational churches are moving toward a one-world religion. If I thought I was a Christian, and I already believe that there is more than one way to heaven, that God and Allah are the same, then why not accept Allah? If we were in the middle of a horrible World War III (terrible things were happening, even nuclear bombs) and a leader came along, and said he would end the war and cause radicals to stop killing, if we would just accept the peaceful Islam, then why not? I have actually seen on television, billboards that say, "Jesus is in the Quran." Below this, it says, "Abraham, Moses, Jesus, Mohammed." This is trying to show a commonality between Christianity and Islam. True believers, of course, will not accept any of this. The Jesus in the Quran is not Jesus, the anointed one, the Son of God. The Quran teaches that God has no son.

According to the Bible, Mary conceived Jesus by the Holy Ghost (Spirit). The Holy Spirit (the Word) became a seed (a sperm) in Mary, and that seed united with an egg. This is what conception means. Jesus is the only begotten of God. His Father is God. The bloodline comes through the father. Jesus has no earthly father. His lineage to David comes through Mary, but His bloodline is through the Father. He is literally God's Son.

As the time gets closer, there will be fewer and fewer true believers and true Bible-believing churches. Jesus even asked when He returns would he find faith on the earth? (Luke 18:8.) There may come a time very soon that in many churches, because of the apostasy, true believers have long left the church. It may be that Jesus could come on a Sunday morning, and in these churches, the people will not even know the rapture has taken place until they go to get their children out of children's church. Ichabod (the Spirit of God has departed) could be written on many churches by this time. How easy it will be for the Antichrist to come into power when it is his time.

It does not have to be that the church has to be raptured for the Antichrist to come forth. I have wondered, and I ask the question because I do not understand the reasoning behind this: "What makes anyone think that the church could keep the Antichrist from coming forth?" The church in America can't even keep America straight. One person stopped prayer in the schools. Did the church stop that? Over fifty-five million babies have been murdered in America. The womb is the most unsafe place in America today. More than one out of five Americans are killed in the womb. Did we stop that? Now even body parts are being sold, and we cannot even get it unfunded. America is the one that has desecrated marriage, and the rainbow (God's covenant not to destroy the whole earth with a flood.) Where is the church stopping all of this? As far as the rest of the world, I have heard that there is a great revival in the underground church in China. But look at what I just wrote. The church is still underground. There were churches in Russia. Did they stop the Bolshevik Revolution and the coming of Communism with its persecution on the church? Look at Romania, Bulgaria, Poland, Czechoslovakia, Hungary, Albania, Yugoslavia—seventy years of religious persecution, and people imprisoned and tortured for their faith in Jesus. Did the church stop all of that? We have had world wars. Hitler had to be stopped with a war. I am sure people were praying, but it still took a world war. Earlier, two-thirds of Europe was wiped out with a plague. Where was the church? If the church is supposed to have authority to stop these things, it is not exercising it. You may add, it isn't about the church, but the Holy Spirit in the church. Well, I have a question, "When the church is raptured, where is the Holy Spirit *going*?" The Holy Spirit (the Spirit of God) is everywhere present. He isn't *going* anywhere. There will be two prophets prophesying during the Tribulation period. How can they prophecy without the Spirit of God? In addition, Revelation 14:13 says that there will be those who will die in the Lord. How can they be in the Lord without the Holy Spirit? (Here is one of those reference in Revelation to the church even though the word, "church" is not used.) Neither point makes a case for a pre-trib rapture. I just do not see that the Bible is telling us that the church would stop the Antichrist when it is time for him to come forth.

Along with this, there may very well be things that hit America because she has pushed God away and committed awful sins, even before a rapture or the Great Tribulation. We are living on borrowed time. The last final straw will be how we treat Israel. Trouble could hit America that has nothing to do with the rapture. Yet the mindset of many in the church is that they will be raptured out before any trouble. We can be very grateful that at the writing of this text, we have a president that supports Israel.

If trouble does come to America, we do not need to live in fear. We just need to be aware that something could hit America before the church is raptured. We need to watch, pray, and be ready because a great harvest of souls could occur. There may be people flocking to Bible-believing churches for help and salvation. We may be here for this time to stand strong and cause people to be saved—great light, in great darkness to get many people turned to God before the Great Tribulation and before the wrath of God comes on the earth.

THE WRATH OF GOD

1 Thessalonians 1:10

10 *And to wait for his Son from heaven*, whom he raised from the dead, even Jesus, *which delivered us from the wrath to come.*

1 Thessalonians 2:19

19 For what is our hope, or joy, or crown of rejoicing? Are not even ye in the presence of our Lord Jesus Christ at his coming?

1 Thessalonians 3:13

13 To the end he may stablish your hearts unblameable in holiness before God, even our Father, at the coming of our Lord Jesus Christ with all his saints.

1 Thessalonians 5:2 -3, 9, 10, 23

2 For yourselves know perfectly that the day of the Lord so cometh as a thief in the night.

3 For when they shall say, Peace and safety; then sudden destruction cometh upon them, as travail upon a woman with child; and they shall not escape.

9 *For God hath not appointed us to wrath, but to obtain salvation by our Lord Jesus Christ,*

10 Who died for us, that, whether we wake or sleep, we should live together with him.

23 And the very God of peace sanctify you wholly; and I pray God your whole spirit and soul and body be preserved blameless unto the coming of our Lord Jesus Christ.

2 Thessalonians 1: 7 – 9

7   And to you who are troubled rest with us, *when the Lord Jesus shall be revealed from heaven* with his mighty angels,

8   *In flaming fire taking vengeance on them that know not God,* and that obey not the gospel of our Lord Jesus Christ:

9   Who shall be punished with *everlasting destruction from the presence of the Lord,* and from the glory of his power;

Romans 1:18

18   For the wrath of God is revealed from heaven against all ungodliness and unrighteousness of men, who hold the truth in unrighteousness;

Romans 2: 5 – 10

5   But after thy hardness and impenitent heart treasurest up unto thyself wrath *against the day of wrath* and revelation of the righteous judgment of God;

6   *Who will render to every man according to his deeds*:

7   To them who by patient continuance in well doing seek for glory and honour and immortality, eternal life:

8   But unto them that are contentious, and do not obey the truth, but obey unrighteousness, indignation and wrath,

9   Tribulation and anguish, upon every soul of man that doeth evil, of the Jew first, and also of the Gentile;

10   But glory, honour, and peace, to every man that worketh good, to the Jew first, and also to the Gentile:

Ephesians 5:6

6   Let no man deceive you with vain words: for
    because of these things cometh the wrath of
    God upon the children of disobedience.

One of the strong points made for a pre-trib rapture is that believers are not appointed to the wrath of God. This idea is that we would have to be taken out of the world to avoid His wrath during the Tribulation period. Is this the only way to avoid God's wrath? Can God keep His own here on earth? We will see later in discussing Revelation that God "sealed" people to preserve them from destruction that was about to occur. What time in the sequence of end time events will be considered the wrath of God?

As you read through these scriptures, such as 1 Thessalonians 1:10 that states, "Wait for His Son from heaven . . . which delivered us from the wrath to come." This speaks to being delivered from the wrath, which will come in the presence of Jesus *after He comes*. First Thessalonians 1:7–9 brings out that when the Lord is revealed from heaven, He shall take vengeance on those who don't know God with destruction from the presence of Jesus. These scriptures are saying that we are not subject to His judgment at His coming. In Revelation, Jesus, at the battle of Armageddon, with the sword (Word) of His mouth, will place those whom He destroys into the "winepress of the wrath of God." According to post-trib teaching, the church will have just been raptured and will not be subject to this wrath. I will show later, two times in Revelation, that it is when this winepress comes, the comment is made, "*Now* has come the wrath of God."

In either case, believers are not subject to the wrath of God. The wrath of God falls on the children of disobedience. There will be a "day of wrath," and the righteous are not subject to it.

In 1 Thessalonians 3:13, it says Jesus is coming with all His saints. If there is a pre-trib rapture, He will come with all those who are in heaven because they would have been raptured and gone to heaven for the years of tribulation. If the rapture is post-trib, He will come with the "dead in Christ" whose spirit went to heaven when they died. Those who are still alive will be caught up to meet them in the air and Jesus will come down to earth with all of them.

Romans 1:18, 2:5–10 and Ephesians 5:6 are more scriptures concerning wrath and seem to support that the wrath is referring to the day of wrath that is part of God's judgment, and not necessarily referring to the time of the Great Tribulation. Jesus stated that in the world, we will have Tribulation (John 16:33), and the Great Tribulation will be the worst ever.

THE ESCAPE CLAUSE

Luke 21:36

> 36 Watch ye therefore, and pray always, that ye may be accounted worthy to escape all these things that shall come to pass, and to stand before the Son of man.

Jesus said this after He explained the events that will occur and the sign of His coming. This could mean that believers will escape the judgment when we stand before Him. The word in Strong's Concordance is to flee from or to get away from. If you look at it just the way it is worded, a good way to escape these things would be to be raptured before they happen. I wonder, however, why we would have to "pray" to escape, if believers are going to be raptured. Do we have to pray, "God, let me go up in the rapture?" Unless you believe in a partial rapture, all who are born of His Spirit will go up in the rapture. A born-again believer is alive unto God spiritually and will go up in the rapture just like he would go to heaven, if he died.

This is one of the scriptures that I am not satisfied with what I know about it at this point. I could make conjectures about it, but I believe there is more to it.

Pre-Trib/Post-trib Rapture Table

Rapture: Coming of the Lord and gathering together of the body of Christ, including dead and living in new resurrected bodies.

Pre-Tribulation (Scriptures supporting a Pre-Trib rapture.)	Pending (Scriptures that need more verifying before placement.)	Post-tribulation (Scriptures supporting a Post-Trib rapture.)
		I Thess 4:13 – 18
		John 6:40, 44, 54
	<2 Thess 2	2 Thess 2
I Thess 5:10 Wrath		I Thess 5:10 Wrath

I have placed 2 Thessalonians 2 (the scripture about restraining) in the post-trib column because as written, it supports a post-trib rapture. There are still others that remain convinced that it fits pre-trib teaching. Paul did not specifically say who the "he" is that restrains.

I put the wrath scriptures and the escape scripture in both columns because it depends on how these scriptures are viewed. If we establish that the wrath is referring to the winepress at Jesus' coming, or that we can be kept if wrath occurs during the Great Tribulation, it will fit the post-trib teaching. The "escape clause," fits strongly in the pre-trib column, although being kept during the tribulation is still a way to escape. Noah was kept in the flood, not taken away from the earth.

Can you see my point about being willing to be open to what God wants to tell us? We need to try to recognize when our own preconceived ideas make us frame the scripture to fit our own viewpoint.

CHAPTER 3

Letters to the Churches

As we start in the book of Revelation, I reemphasize that I do not think that I know all there is to know about this book. In fact, the more I read, the more I see I need to learn. This is a part of the fascination with the Word of God. No matter how many times you read a scripture, there is more to learn. God's ways are higher than our ways. The wisdom of the Spirit of God is limitless.

Isaiah 55:9

9   For as the heavens are higher than the earth,
    so are my ways higher than your ways, and
    my thoughts than your thoughts.

Revelation 1:1 – 9

1   The Revelation of Jesus Christ, which God
    gave unto him, to shew unto his servants
    things which must shortly come to pass; and
    he sent and signified it by his angel unto his
    servant John:

2   Who bare record of the word of God, and of
    the testimony of Jesus Christ, and of all things
    that he saw.

3   Blessed is he that readeth, and they that hear
    the words of this prophecy, and keep those
    things which are written therein: for the time
    is at hand.

4   John to the seven churches which are in Asia:
    Grace be unto you, and peace, from him which

is, and which was, and which is to come; and from the seven Spirits which are before his throne;

5 And from Jesus Christ, who is the faithful witness, and the first begotten of the dead, and the prince of the kings of the earth. Unto him that loved us, and washed us from our sins in his own blood,

6 And hath made us kings and priests unto God and his Father; to him be glory and dominion for ever and ever. Amen.

7 Behold, he cometh with clouds; and every eye shall see him, and they also which pierced him: and all kindreds of the earth shall wail because of him. Even so, Amen.

8 I am Alpha and Omega, the beginning and the ending, saith the Lord, which is, and which was, and which is to come, the Almighty.

9 I John, who also am your brother, and companion in tribulation, and in the kingdom and patience of Jesus Christ, was in the isle that is called Patmos, for the word of God, and for the testimony of Jesus Christ.

Acts 1:9-11

9 And when he had spoken these things, while they beheld, he was taken up; and a cloud received him out of their sight.

10 And while they looked stedfastly toward heaven as he went up, behold, two men stood by them in white apparel;

11 Which also said, Ye men of Galilee, why stand ye gazing up into heaven? this same Jesus, which is taken up from you into heaven, shall so come in like manner as ye have seen him go into heaven.

This book is the Revelation of Jesus Christ. What is wonderful about this book, no matter how horrible much of it will seem, we know the ending. It is a victorious ending for those who are in Christ. This is the revelation of Jesus and His victory over Satan and death. It is Revelation—singular, not plural. I have already addressed the fact that we are blessed, if we read this book.

Verse 4. We see seven churches and seven Spirits of God. We are going to see many seven's in Revelation. (Seven churches, seven Spirits of God, seven seals, seven trumpets, seven vials, seven eyes, seven horns). Seven in the scriptures is a word meaning completion, perfection, and one I don't hear as often is rest. I heard an explanation regarding numbers that the way to understand the meaning of a number is that the first time it is mentioned in scripture, whatever it is referring to in that scripture will be its meaning throughout the Bible. I haven't researched this for all numbers, but seven, for example, refers to the seventh day of creation when God had completed all His creation. It was good, and He rested from His works. On the sixth day, He created man, and six is the number of man in scripture.

I wondered about the seven churches in Asia. I can understand the significance of the number seven, but why churches in Asia? I read in a commentary that the particular churches are those for which John had oversight as an apostle. This made sense to me. If Jesus were going to give an apostle a message to the church, it makes sense that He would have the apostle tell all the churches in his care.

I have speculated about the seven spirits. We will see this terminology a few more times in Revelation. Again, we see the number seven. At one point the seven Spirits are seen as seven flames of lamps before the throne. John sees seven eyes on the lamb that are the seven Spirits that go throughout the earth. Some say that the seven Spirits are the seven-fold Spirit of God and can describe seven characteristics of the Spirit of God. This could be possible, but I am sure if it had said ten Spirits that we could come up with ten characteristics of the Spirit of God. If this represents the Holy Spirit, I still don't see why it is divided into seven or seven-fold spirits. Solomon's temple had a lamp with seven bowls. The Jewish menorah is has seven bowls for seven candles. This may just be continuing the symbolism of seven and lamps to represent His Spirit.

Verse 7. "Behold He comes with clouds, and every eye shall see Him." There are two ways Jesus comes with clouds. He comes with His saints, and in Hebrews 12:1, we see a reference to those that have gone on as "clouds of witnesses." In addition, Jesus went up in a cloud, and He is returning in a cloud (Acts 1:9–11). It says that every eye shall see Him when He comes. This is referring to the coming at the end of the Tribulation period. We will cover the scripture in Matthew 24 that says His coming will be as the lightning shines from the east to the west. This also states that even those that pierced Him will see Him. Those that specifically pierced Him are not alive. I do not know if this just refers to the "people group" responsible for His crucifixion or if it could mean that the event will be so dramatic, even people in hell will be able to see His coming.

All kindreds are going to wail because He is coming to end the battle with the winepress of the wrath of God and will destroy those that fought against Him and Israel. He will then set up His kingdom. He will take over the nations. They will become His, and He will rule with a rod of iron. Those who went up in the rapture will rule and reign with Him as overcomers.

Verse 8. Alpha and omega are Greek first and last letters for beginning and end as our alphabet is A–Z.

Verse 9. John was exiled to Patmos.

Revelation 1:10 – 20

10 I was in the Spirit on the Lord's day, and heard behind me a great voice, as of a trumpet,

11 Saying, I am Alpha and Omega, the first and the last: and, What thou seest, write in a book, and send it unto the seven churches which are in Asia; unto Ephesus, and unto Smyrna, and unto Pergamos, and unto Thyatira, and unto Sardis, and unto Philadelphia, and unto Laodicea.

12 And I turned to see the voice that spake with me. And being turned, I saw seven golden candlesticks;

13 And in the midst of the seven candlesticks one like unto the Son of man, clothed with a garment down to the foot, and girt about the paps with a golden girdle.

14 His head and his hairs were white like wool, as white as snow; and his eyes were as a flame of fire;

15 And his feet like unto fine brass, as if they burned in a furnace; and his voice as the sound of many waters.

16 And he had in his right hand seven stars: and out of his mouth a sharp twoedged sword: and his countenance was as the sun shineth in his strength.

17 And when I saw him, I fell at his feet as dead. And he laid his right hand upon me, saying unto me, Fear not; I am the first and the last:

18 I am he that liveth, and was dead; and, behold, I am alive for evermore, Amen; and have the keys of hell and of death.

19 Write the things which thou hast seen, and the things which are, and the things which shall be hereafter;

20 The mystery of the seven stars which thou sawest in my right hand, and the seven golden candlesticks. The seven stars are the angels of the seven churches: and the seven candlesticks which thou sawest are the seven churches.

Verse 10. John was in the Spirit, and he was shown things. He describes the voice as a trumpet. In other places, the sound will be described as the sound of many waters or thunder. It could be that this is a loud, booming sound. If it were today, John might describe the sound as a jet taking off or a rock concert.

Verse 11. The seven churches are listed. He sees seven golden candlesticks (or lampstands. They were oil lamps in that day, not wax candles). Verse 20 tells us the candlesticks represent the seven churches.

Verse 13. Jesus (the son of Man) is in the midst of the candlesticks. It is wonderful to know that Jesus is in the midst of churches.

Verses 14–15. John describes Jesus with head and hair white, eyes a flame of fire, feet as brass burned in a furnace. His voice, the sound of many waters. Perhaps this is what he looked like in the transfiguration (Matthew 17:2). This was a moment when apostles saw Jesus changed and looked white and he was talking with Moses and Elijah.

Verse 16. Jesus had seven stars in His right hand. Verse 20 tells us the stars are the angels of the churches. Strong's Concordance says the word angel is messenger or by implication, a pastor. It is great to know that Jesus has the pastor in His right hand.

Out of His mouth went a sharp two-edged sword. We have discussed previously that the sword represents the Word.

Hebrews 4:12

> 12 For the word of God is quick, and powerful, and sharper than any twoedged sword, piercing even to the dividing asunder of soul and spirit, and of the joints and marrow, and is a discerner of the thoughts and intents of the heart.

All the way through Revelation, we will see that the sword is in His mouth. We have already seen that the sword is powerful Word. This is important because I have heard it taught that when Jesus comes, He will actually fight in the battle of Armageddon with a real sword in His hand and get bloody and that those who were in the rapture will fight with Him. I asked myself, "What are we going to be, swashbucklers like Robin Hood and his merry men?" This is why it can be so good to be familiar with scripture so that when you hear something like that, you will know it just isn't right. You can see that there is something wrong with that because it says the sword is in His mouth. Why would Jesus have to come and fight with a sword? Is it going to be made out of tungsten? Even in the Old Testament, when God fought for Israel, the enemy might be destroyed by hail or hornets. God did not have to literally kill with a sword.

Verse 17. John falls at Jesus' feet as dead. This is a common reaction in scripture when someone is in the presence of an angel or Jesus. The powerful spiritual presence can weaken or put such fear that it pulls a person down. Then comes the wording, "Fear not."

Verse 18. He has the keys of hell and death. When Jesus rose, He gained victory over hell and death.

I Corinthians 15: 55 – 57

55 O death, where is thy sting? O grave, where is thy victory?

56 The sting of death is sin; and the strength of sin is the law.

57 But thanks be to God, which giveth us the victory through our Lord Jesus Christ.

Verse 19. John is told he will see things past, present, and future. In Revelation 2 and 3, when given messages to the churches, he is told what the churches did, ("I know your works"), what they were doing presently, and what would happen in the future. In Revelation 4, he is then told he will be shown things that are "hereafter" (in the future). From Revelation 4 on he is seeing things that are future.

Verse 20. As stated earlier, John is given the explanation of what the seven candlesticks and stars are. Often, even when John sees things that don't make sense, as you read on, you will be given an explanation of what is actually being seen. If something seems strange, sometimes, just hold on and you can get an explanation. The explanation may even be a couple of chapters later.

Revelation 2: 1 – 11

1   Unto the angel of the church of Ephesus write; These things saith he that holdeth the seven stars in his right hand, who walketh in the midst of the seven golden candlesticks;

2   I know thy works, and thy labour, and thy patience, and how thou canst not bear them which are evil: and thou hast tried them which say they are apostles, and are not, and hast found them liars:

3   And hast borne, and hast patience, and for my name's sake hast laboured, and hast not fainted.

4   Nevertheless I have somewhat against thee, because thou hast left thy first love.

5   Remember therefore from whence thou art fallen, and repent, and do the first works; or else I will come unto thee quickly, and will remove thy candlestick out of his place, except thou repent.

6   But this thou hast, that thou hatest the deeds of the Nicolaitans, which I also hate.

7   He that hath an ear, let him hear what the Spirit saith unto the churches; to him that overcometh will I give to eat of the tree of life, which is in the midst of the paradise of God.

8   And unto the angel of the church in Smyrna write; these things saith the first and the last, which was dead, and is alive;

9   I know thy works, and tribulation, and poverty, (but thou art rich) and I know the blasphemy of them which say they are Jews, and are not, but are the synagogue of Satan.

10 Fear none of those things which thou shalt suffer: behold, the Devil shall cast some of you

into prison, that ye may be tried; and ye shall have tribulation ten days: be thou faithful unto death, and I will give thee a crown of life.

11 He that hath an ear, let him hear what the Spirit saith unto the churches; He that overcometh shall not be hurt of the second death.

Revelation 2–3 are written to the seven churches. I am not going to go over the churches in detail. This could entail a whole book. I heard a little bit on a teaching, explaining that what Jesus wrote to each church had relevance to that particular city. For example, in Laodicea, the last church referenced, the city was famous for medicine, specifically eye salve. In addition, their water could only be drank hot or ice cold because when it was lukewarm, it was nauseating. These are items that Jesus used to explain to the Laodiceans what their spiritual condition was.

Verse 6. Jesus says he hates the deeds of the Nicolaitans. What I can gather from things I have read about this is that this doctrine seemed to flow with the Gnostic doctrine. The word Gnostic comes from the word meaning "knowing." Its teaching was that in your body you can sin, but your spirit is saved, and in order to know and understand sin, it is important to experience it. Wouldn't that make serving God pleasurable to the flesh? Of course, the Word teaches us that yielding to sin puts us into bondage.

Romans 6:16

16 Know ye not, that to whom ye yield yourselves servants to obey, his servants ye are to whom ye obey; whether of sin unto death, or of obedience unto righteousness?

Romans 8:13

13 For if ye live after the flesh, ye shall die: but if ye through the Spirit do mortify the deeds of the body, ye shall live.

This explains one of the reasons He hated this doctrine. Some of the books that you hear about that have been found called the "lost gospels" tout this teaching. Be careful about books outside the Bible. Even in early days of the church, there were false doctrines and teachings.

Verse 7. The main points I want to discuss are the passages that address overcoming. Verse 7 states, "He that hath an ear (meaning a spiritual ear), let him hear what the Spirit says unto the churches." Churches is plural not singular, and "he that hath an ear" refers to anyone who will listen to what the Spirit is saying. All the "overcoming" scriptures, I believe, apply to all believers. We overcome by the blood of the lamb and the word of our testimony (Rev. 12:11), so these apply to us. The first overcome statement was given to the church at Ephesus. It will be granted to the overcomer to eat of the tree of life in the paradise of God. The tree of life was in the Garden of Eden, and when Adam and Eve disobeyed God, cherubim were placed before the tree of life to keep them from being able to eat of it and live forever in the state they were in. This tree is now in the paradise of God. I feel this tree is a type of Jesus. He is the life (John 14:6). We will see this tree mentioned some more in Revelation. Whether there is an actual tree remains to be seen.

Verse 11. To the church of Smyrna, we are told that the overcomer will not be hurt of the second death. We will learn later in Revelation that the second death is the judgment at the white throne of God in which those not found in the Book of Life of the Lamb will be cast into the Lake of Fire. Those who receive a resurrected body in the rapture, which is called the first resurrection, do not face this Great White Throne Judgment (Rev. 20:11–15). This judgment occurs after the thousand-year reign.

Revelation 2:12 – 17

12 And to the angel of the church in Pergamos write; These things saith he which hath the sharp sword with two edges;

13 I know thy works, and where thou dwellest, even where Satan's seat is: thou holdest fast

my name, and hast not denied my faith, even in those days wherein Antipas was my faithful martyr, who was slain among you, where Satan dwelleth.

14 But I have a few things against thee, because thou hast there them that hold the doctrine of Balaam, who taught Balac to cast a stumblingblock before the children of Israel, to eat things sacrificed unto idols, and to commit fornication.

15 So hast thou also them that hold the doctrine of the Nicolaitans, which thing I hate.

16 Repent; or else I will come unto thee quickly, and will fight against them with the sword of my mouth.

17 He that hath an ear, let him hear what the Spirit saith unto the churches; To him that overcometh will I give to eat of the hidden manna, and will give him a white stone, and in the stone a new name written, which no man knoweth saving he that receiveth it.

The third church is Pergamos (Pergamum in other translations). Verse 13 states that Pergamos is where Satan's seat is. Pergamos was in what is now Turkey. There was at one time an altar and throne to the god, Zeus. This altar was taken to Germany, and Hitler made speeches with this throne in the background. When you think of the satanic force behind Hitler, it is very telling. Turkey wants this back and, I understand, is building another one. It may be good to keep our eye on Turkey in this last day and where the old altar of Zeus resides.

Verse 17. The overcomer will be given hidden manna to eat and will be given a white stone with a new name written. Jesus said He is the manna (bread) from heaven (John 6:31, 41). The word manna means, "What is it?" When the Israelites were in the wilderness God gave them a substance to eat that appeared in the morning with the dew. The Israelites did not know what it was so they called it manna. God gave manna to the Israelites to eat for the forty years they were in the wilderness.

I saw in commentary that a white stone was used as we would use a ticket today to get into a coliseum. That makes sense.

Are you curious as to what your new name is?

Revelation 2: 18 – 29

18 And unto the angel of the church in Thyatira write; These things saith the Son of God, who hath his eyes like unto a flame of fire, and his feet are like fine brass;

19 I know thy works, and charity, and service, and faith, and thy patience, and thy works; and the last to be than the first.

20 Notwithstanding I have a few things against thee, because thou sufferest that woman Jezebel, which calleth a prophetess, to teach and to seduce my servants to commit fornication, and to eat things sacrificed unto idols.

21 And I gave her space to repent of her fornication; and she repented not.

22 Behold, I will cast her into a bed, and them that commit adultery with her into great tribulation, except they repent of their deeds.

23 And I will kill her children with death; and all the churches shall know that I am he which searcheth the reins and hearts: and I will give unto every one of you according to your works.

24 But unto you I say, and unto the rest in Thyatira, as many as have not this doctrine, and which have not known the depths of

Satan, as they speak; I will put upon you none other burden.

25 But that which ye have already hold fast till I come.

26 And he that overcometh, and keepeth my works unto the end, to him will I give power over the nations:

27 And he shall rule them with a rod of iron; as the vessels of a potter shall they be broken to shivers: even as I received of my Father.

28 And I will give him the morning star.

29 He that hath an ear, let him hear what the Spirit saith unto the churches.

Verses 26 – 27. To Thyatira, the fourth overcome is that we will be given power over the nations to rule with a rod of iron and will be given the morning star. (A reference to Jesus. He is the bright and morning star [Rev. 22:16]). We were told that Jesus rules with a rod of iron in Revelation 12:15 and 19:15, so we, too, will rule with Him with a rod of iron.

Revelation 3: 1 – 12

1 And unto the angel of the church in Sardis write; These things saith he that hath the seven Spirits of God, and the seven stars; I know thy works, that thou hast a name that thou livest, and art dead.

2 Be watchful, and strengthen the things which remain, that are ready to die: for I have not found thy works perfect before God.

3 Remember therefore how thou hast received and heard, and hold fast, and repent. If therefore thou shalt not watch, I will come on thee as a thief, and thou shalt not know what hour I will come upon thee.

4   Thou hast a few names even in Sardis which have not defiled their garments; and they shall walk with me in white: for they are worthy.

5   He that overcometh, the same shall be clothed in white raiment; and I will not blot out his name out of the book of life, but I will confess his name before my Father, and before his angels.

6   He that hath an ear, let him hear what the Spirit saith unto the churches.

7   And to the angel of the church in Philadelphia write; These things saith he that is holy, he that is true, he that hath the key of David, he that openeth, and no man shutteth; and shutteth, and no man openeth;

8   I know thy works: behold, I have set before thee an open door, and no man can shut it: for thou hast a little strength, and hast kept my word, and hast not denied my name.

9   Behold, I will make them of the synagogue of Satan, which say they are Jews and are not, but do lie; behold, I will make them to come and worship before thy feet, and to know that I have loved thee.

10 Because thou hast kept the word of my patience, I also will keep thee from the hour of temptation, which shall come upon all the world, to try them that dwell upon the earth.

11 Behold, I come quickly: hold that fast which thou hast, that no man take thy crown.

12 Him that overcometh will I make a pillar in the temple of my God, and he shall go no more out: and I will write upon him the name of my God, and the name of the city of my God, which is new Jerusalem, which cometh

down out of heaven from my God: and I will
write upon him my new name.

Verse 5. The fifth church is Sardis. The overcomer is to be clothed
in white raiment, our name will not be blotted out of the Book of
Life, and Jesus will confess our name before God and the angels.

Verses 6 – 12. The sixth church is Philadelphia (brotherly love).
The overcomer will be a pillar in the temple and will have the name
of God, the name of the city of God, New Jerusalem, and Jesus' new
name written on him. Did you know that Jesus is going to have a
new name? We saw earlier that we are given a new name, and now
we see that Jesus is given a new name. As highly as His name is
regarded now, imagine Him having a new name. When John sees
Jesus in a vision concerning His' coming, it says that Jesus has a
name that no man knows (Rev. 19:12). That is because He is given a
new name. There is no reason to speculate on it because no man can
know it now.

In verse 10 it states that because they kept the word, He would
keep them from the hour of temptation, which will come upon all the
world. This is another place that many people claim is the rapture. It
is said that in order to be kept, we must be raptured out. This is not
the case. Being raptured is one way we can be kept, but it is not the
only way. In John 17:15, when Jesus is praying, He asks God to keep
his disciples from the evil and says He doesn't mean to take them
out of the world but keep them. This scripture isn't referring to the
rapture, but I want you to look at the terminology. The phrase "keep
from" does not necessarily mean that you have to be taken out of
the world. We can be kept in tribulation. It depends on how you look
at this scripture and what your perspective is.

John 17: 15

15 I pray not that thou shouldest take them out
of the world, but that thou shouldest keep
them from the evil.

Some have said that Noah's ark is a type of rapture. Noah and his
family were raptured out of the flood. It could also be that it shows that

Noah and his family were kept in the flood. They didn't get raptured out of the earth; they were kept. They went through the flood and survived. Had the other people believed, they could have been kept too. You would have thought that after all the years that Noah built the ark and warned people that someone would have listened to Noah. But no one did. In reference to being kept in the flood instead of being taken out, they heard the rain; they floated on the waters for days and had to wait for the waters to subside. When they got out of the ark, no one was left, not parents, grandparents, cousins, uncles, or friends. Everyone else was gone except for eight people.

This next point is extra. (Or, as I used to tell students when I added something or digressed, "This won't cost you anything.") Did you know that Methuselah, the oldest known man (he lived to be 969 years, Gen. 1397 5:27) died the year of the flood? You can calculate this by the details in the scripture. Methuselah was Noah's grandfather. We don't know if he died in the flood, but he did die the year of the flood.

Revelation 3: 14 – 22

14 And unto the angel of the church of the Laodiceans write; These things saith the Amen, the faithful and true witness, the beginning of the creation of God;

15 I know thy works, that thou art neither cold nor hot: I would thou wert cold or hot.

16 So then because thou art lukewarm, and neither cold nor hot, I will spue thee out of my mouth.

17 Because thou sayest, I am rich, and increased with goods, and have need of nothing; and knowest not that thou art wretched, and miserable, and poor, and blind, and naked:

18 I counsel thee to buy of me gold tried in the fire, that thou mayest be rich; and white raiment, that thou mayest be clothed, and that the shame of thy nakedness do not

appear; and anoint thine eyes with eyesalve, that thou mayest see.

19 As many as I love, I rebuke and chasten: be zealous therefore, and repent.

20 Behold, I stand at the door, and knock: if any man hear my voice, and open the door, I will come in to him, and will sup with him, and he with me.

21 To him that overcometh will I grant to sit with me in my throne, even as I also overcame, and am set down with my Father in his throne.

22 He that hath an ear, let him hear what the Spirit saith unto the churches.

The seventh church is Laodicea.

Verse 17. Addresses the fact that the church was rich in goods and yet Jesus said they were poor and wretched toward the things of God. Jesus told the Smyrna church He knew they were poor in physical things but rich in God. (Revelation 2:9)

Verse 21. The overcomer will sit on the throne with Jesus as He sits with God on His throne. We sit on thrones with God. That is a mighty big throne. Isaiah 66:1 says heaven is God's throne and the earth is His footstool.

Isaiah 66:1

66 Thus saith the Lord, The heaven is my throne, and the earth is my footstool: where is the house that ye build unto me? and where is the place of my rest?

A throne represents authority. Jesus told the twelve apostles that they would sit on thrones judging the twelve tribes of Israel (Matthew 19:28). In Revelation 22:3, it states that the throne of God and the Lamb (Jesus) will be on the new earth. Whether there will be literal thrones remains to be seen. The throne may represent authority, or there could be literal thrones. Either way, the overcomer will rule with Jesus.

Some have framed these churches as church ages. The first being Ephesus and the last age today is Laodicea. It seems most no longer hold to this teaching. These were existing churches in John's day, and we can learn from what Jesus told them. Jesus addressed what was going on in the churches, and He said for everyone to pay attention to what happens when you overcome. "He that hath and ear, let him hear what the Spirit says."

Revelation 12: 11

11 And they overcame him by the blood of the Lamb, and by the word of their testimony.

In summary, these are what overcomers will obtain:

1. Be able to eat of the tree of life in the midst of the paradise of God.
2. Will not be hurt of the second death.
3. Will eat of the hidden manna and be given a new name.
4. Will rule and reign with a rod of iron and be given the morning star.
5. Will be clothed in white raiment; name will not be blotted out of the book of life and Jesus will confess your name before God and the angels.
6. Will be made a pillar in the temple of God and have the name of God and the New Jerusalem written on you.
7. Will sit with Jesus on his throne even as Jesus is sitting with His father on His throne.

CHAPTER 4

The Seven Seals

Revelation 4

1   After this I looked, and, behold, a door was opened in heaven: and the first voice which I heard was as it were of a trumpet talking with me; which said, Come up hither, and I will shew thee things which must be hereafter.

2   And immediately I was in the spirit: and, behold, a throne was set in heaven, and one sat on the throne.

3   And he that sat was to look upon like a jasper and a sardine stone: and there was a rainbow round about the throne, in sight like unto an emerald.

4   And round about the throne were four and twenty seats: and upon the seats I saw four and twenty elders sitting, clothed in white raiment; and they had on their heads crowns of gold.

5   And out of the throne proceeded lightnings and thunderings and voices: and there were seven lamps of fire burning before the throne, which are the seven Spirits of God.

6   And before the throne there was a sea of glass like unto crystal: and in the midst of the

throne, and round about the throne, were four beasts full of eyes before and behind.

7   And the first beast was like a lion, and the second beast like a calf, and the third beast had a face as a man, and the fourth beast was like a flying eagle.

8   And the four beasts had each of them six wings about him; and they were full of eyes within: and they rest not day and night, saying, Holy, holy, holy, Lord God Almighty, which was, and is, and is to come.

9   And when those beasts give glory and honour and thanks to him that sat on the throne, who liveth for ever and ever,

10 The four and twenty elders fall down before him that sat on the throne, and worship him that liveth for ever and ever, and cast their crowns before the throne, saying,

11 Thou art worthy, O Lord, to receive glory and honour and power: for thou hast created all things, and for thy pleasure they are and were created.

At this point Jesus has finished addressing the churches. As noted previously, some say that because the word "church" is not mentioned anymore that the church has been raptured. There are references to saints (Re. 14:12) and those who "die in the Lord." It is just that He is finished writing letters to the churches. There are still believers addressed throughout Revelation. Since there are still believers on the earth during the Tribulation period, the fact that the word "church" is not mentioned after Revelation 3 is irrelevant. Some more circular reasoning that is a misconception. It has no bearing on whether the rapture is pre- or post-tribulation. In addition, as I discussed previously, if one holds to the idea that because the word "church" not being used means the church will not experience what is discussed, then it would follow that because the word, "church" is not mentioned in a single scripture concerning the rapture, that the church will not be raptured. Obviously not the case.

Verse 4. John is told to "come up hither," and he would be shown things, which must come hereafter (in the future). We have already discussed that John was in the spirit; he did not get raptured. The events occurring at the rapture do not present at this point in Revelation. There is not a coming of Jesus nor a resurrection of the dead in Christ, neither does John put on a resurrected body. He is in the spirit and comes back to earth alive to write about it.

He sees visions in heaven. He describes the throne.

Verse 5. Around about the throne were twenty-four seats and twenty-four elders sitting clothed in white raiment. Some have said that these represent the twelve tribes of Israel and the twelve apostles sitting on thrones. These will be mentioned again. As with the number seven, we will see many twelves and multiples of twelve. The number twelve refers to government and government authority. These could represent all of us eventually, since we were told the overcomer would sit on thrones, or they could be a specific group given the distinction of being elders. Sometimes, in Revelation, we see something occurring in the throne, in the midst of the throne, or around the throne. This may be a throne area, such as a platform in an auditorium. Some refer to a throne room. In this particular passage, the elders are round about the throne. Remember that Isaiah said that heaven is God's throne. This verse also mentions seven lamps burning before the throne, which are the seven spirits of God that was discussed earlier.

Verses 6–7. There is a sea of glass. We will see that waters represent people, multitudes, and nations (Rev. 17:15). We see four beasts. We will see these creatures many times along with the twenty-four elders. They are full of eyes and have six wings. One had the face of a lion; another, a calf, a man, and an eagle. They worship God constantly. In Ezekiel, at the river Chebar, Ezekiel sees four creatures. They were different in that they only had four wings, and each creature had all four faces. They seem like pretty weird creatures. The faces were the same: lion, ox, man, and an eagle. Later in Ezekiel chapter 10, Ezekiel says these creatures are cherubim. Apparently, cherubim can have four faces or one. Perhaps some have two. I do not know if these descriptions of cherubim are symbolism in the same way John sees a lamb, and we know it represents Jesus, (This will be shown in a later chapter,) or if cherubim really look like this. It would seem that they really do look as John describes them because Ezekiel describes them in almost the same way. However, God can still be showing them to both with symbolism. It may be that they can change shape. Satan was an "anointed cherub" (Ezekiel 28:14) and can be transformed into an angel of light.

2 Corinthians 11:14

14 And no marvel; for Satan himself is transformed into an angel of light.

I heard an explanation that the faces represent categories of animals on the earth. The lion represents wild animals; the calf, domesticated animals; man, of course, man; and the eagle, birds. In the ocean, I guess mammals such as dolphins could be wild or domesticated (as Flipper), and whales could be wild. I wondered why this would matter, but we will see in Revelation 5:13 that when the beasts worship that all creatures on the earth worship. It could be that one of the roles of cherubim is to lead earthly creatures in praise and worship.

Revelation 5

1 And I saw in the right hand of him that sat on the throne a book written within and on the backside, sealed with seven seals.

2 And I saw a strong angel proclaiming with a loud voice, who is worthy to open the book, and to lose the seals thereof?

3 And no man in heaven, nor in earth, neither under the earth, was able to open the book, neither to look thereon.

4 And I wept much, because no man was found worthy to open and to read the book, neither to look thereon.

5   And one of the elders saith unto me, Weep not: behold, the Lion of the tribe of Juda, the Root of David, hath prevailed to open the book, and to lose the seven seals thereof.

6   And I beheld, and, lo, in the midst of the throne and of the four beasts, and in the midst of the elders, stood a Lamb as it had been slain, having seven horns and seven eyes, which the seven Spirits of God are sent forth into all the earth.

7   And he came and took the book out of the right hand of him that sat upon the throne.

8   And when he had taken the book, the four beasts and four and twenty elders fell down before the Lamb, having every one of them harps, and golden vials full of odours, which are the prayers of saints.

9   And they sung a new song, saying, Thou art worthy to take the book, and to open the seals thereof: for thou wast slain, and hast redeemed us to God by thy blood out of every kindred, and tongue, and people, and nation;

10   And hast made us unto our God kings and priests: and we shall reign on the earth.

11   And I beheld, and I heard the voice of many angels round about the throne and the beasts and the elders: and the number of them was ten thousand times ten thousand, and thousands of thousands;

12   Saying with a loud voice, worthy is the Lamb that was slain to receive power, and riches, and wisdom, and strength, and honour, and glory, and blessing.

13   And every creature which is in heaven, and on the earth, and under the earth, and such as

are in the sea, and all that are in them, heard I saying, Blessing, and honour, and glory, and power, be unto him that sitteth upon the throne, and unto the Lamb for ever and ever.

14 And the four beasts said, Amen. And the four and twenty elders fell down and worshipped him that liveth for ever and ever.

We see that God has a book sealed with seven seals, and we find that Jesus is the only one found worthy to open the seals to see what is in the book.

Verse 4. John wept because no man was found worthy to open and read the book. I wonder had he known what was in the book, would he have been so anxious to have it opened?

Verse 5. Jesus is the Lion of the tribe of Judah, the Root of David, and was worthy to open the seven seals. Worthy possibly because He is the Lamb that was slain or because of the fact that He was holy, without spot and sacrificed Himself.

Verse 6. Jesus is that Lamb (John 1:29). He is a Lion and a Lamb. The lamb is described as having seven horns and seven eyes. The eyes are the seven Spirits of God sent forth into all the earth.

Verse 8. The four beasts and twenty-four elders are mentioned. The prayers of saints are a fragrance to God.

Verse 9. This says that the Lamb has redeemed us from every tribe. Who are the "us" since it is the elders and four beasts that are talking? I have seen several commentaries that say that Jesus redeemed men or people instead of "us".

Verse 11. There are millions of angels.

Revelation 6: 1 – 8

1 And I saw when the Lamb opened one of the seals, and I heard, as it were the noise of

thunder, one of the four beasts saying, come and see.

2   And I saw, and behold a white horse: and he that sat on him had a bow; and a crown was given unto him: and he went forth conquering, and to conquer.

3   And when he had opened the second seal, I heard the second beast say, Come and see.

4   And there went out another horse that was red: and power was given to him that sat thereon to take peace from the earth, and that they should kill one another: and there was given unto him a great sword.

5   And when he had opened the third seal, I heard the third beast say, Come and see. And I beheld, and lo a black horse; and he that sat on him had a pair of balances in his hand.

6   And I heard a voice in the midst of the four beasts say, a measure of wheat for a penny, and three measures of barley for a penny; and see thou hurt not the oil and the wine.

7   And when he had opened the fourth seal, I heard the voice of the fourth beast say, come and see.

8   And I looked, and behold a pale horse: and his name that sat on him was Death, and Hell followed with him. And power was given unto them over the fourth part of the earth, to kill with sword, and with hunger, and with death, and with the beasts of the earth.

Revelation 6 shows the Lamb opening six of the seven seals one at a time. As each one is opened, John sees something and describes what he sees. The first four seals are known as the Four Horses of the Apocalypse. (Judgment day or end of the age). The first horse is white, and a conqueror sits on it. The second is red, and the one sitting on him has a sword and power to take peace from the earth. The third is black, and the rider has a pair of balances. The fourth is pale, and death and hell are its riders.

Now what on earth are these four horses? Years ago, when I was reading a "Thompson Chain Reference Bible", as I read about the white horse, it said over to the left in the margin, a conqueror. The red horse had beside it, war. To the side of the black horse was famine. The pale horse was death and hell. These make sense to me, based on the description of the horses.

I have heard different ideas, and I know John sees a vision of Jesus on a horse at His coming. Because of different questions arising, I just asked the Lord, "What is the meaning of a horse in Bible prophecy?" When John saw candlesticks, it was explained what they represented, and what the stars represented. Someone told me that in dreams, a horse is power. That makes sense, you know, horsepower. But what does a horse mean in prophecy? I got an understanding that I have never heard anyone give before. I am not saying it is revelation knowledge, and it is no big deal. I may never have heard anyone discuss this question because it didn't interest anyone. But it interested me, so I asked the question. I saw a scripture in Zechariah and made a connection to the horses in the book of Revelation.

Zechariah 6:1 – 5

1   And I turned, and lifted up mine eyes, and looked, and, behold, there came four chariots out from between two mountains; and the mountains were mountains of brass.

2   In the first chariot were red horses; and in the second chariot black horses;

3   And in the third chariot white horses; and in the fourth chariot grisled and bay horses.

4   Then I answered and said unto the angel that talked with me, what are these, my lord?

5   And the angel answered and said unto me,
these are the four spirits of the heavens, which
go forth from standing before the Lord of all
the earth.

Horses are also mentioned in Zechariah 1, and these horses go to different parts of the earth.

Verses 2–3. Zechariah sees chariots, and in the first chariot were red horses; the second, black horses; the third, white; and the fourth, grisled and bay (or spotted). Do these look familiar? The last is not exactly the same.

Verse 4. Zechariah asks, "What are these?"

Verse 5. The angel said, "These are the four spirits of the heavens, which go forth from standing before all the earth." Over in the margin of the Bible I was reading, for spirit, it said, "Or winds." We know that the word spirit comes from a word meaning "breath" or "wind." When meditating on it this, I thought of a miniseries that was on years ago called "The Winds of War." It was about the build-up in and around the happenings of WWII. I thought about these horses and what they were, and because Zechariah saw them and they were sent forth in the earth, they had been around before. I realized that they are spirits that have been around since the history of mankind. What John is seeing is that all four of these horses will be present during this time in Revelation.

The White Horse (The Conqueror). In seeing these horses as spirits, I ask, "What person in his right mind would want to conquer and rule the world?" It may be a power thing, but even if someone wanted that kind of power, what would make anyone think he could rule the world? Yet we have seen throughout history a spirit of a conqueror wanting to take over the world (Attila the Hun, Napoleon, the Roman Caesars, Russian leaders under Communism, Hitler, and now ISIS, to name a few).

The Red Horse (War). If there is a conqueror, there are going to be those that oppose him and which leads to war. Just like WWII.

The Black Horse (Famine). This can occur with war are refugees and people starving. Just by itself, famine can be a spiritual force. Many times people are starving because of their governments creating the situation, and food can't get to the people. We have seen this, for instance, in Africa. We have enough food to feed the world, but we cannot always get it to people who are displaced because of officials in governments.

The Pale Horse (Death and Hell). (I imagine the grim reaper) Of course, with war comes death from the sword, pestilence (diseases), and famine.

What I gleaned about what horses represent in biblical prophecy is that they represent a happening or a movement, such as war. World War I and II were great happenings. Further in Revelation, as will be discussed, John sees a vision of Jesus coming on a horse. Jesus being seen on a horse at His coming, of course, represents a great event that will be one of the biggest movements in our world. It will completely change things. The nations are going to become His, and we are going to rule and reign with Him for a millennium (a thousand years). These are representations of spiritual forces that produce a happening or major event. No one saw red horses running around during World War I or II.

Revelation 6: 9 – 17

9 And when he had opened the fifth seal, I saw under the altar the souls of them that were slain for the word of God, and for the testimony which they held:

10 And they cried with a loud voice, saying, how long, O Lord, holy and true, dost thou not judge and avenge our blood on them that dwell on the earth?

11 And white robes were given unto every one of them; and it was said unto them, that they should rest yet for a little season, until their fellowservants also and their brethren,

that should be killed as they were, should be fulfilled.

12 And I beheld when he had opened the sixth seal, and, lo, there was a great earthquake; and the sun became black as sackcloth of hair, and the moon became as blood;

13 And the stars of heaven fell unto the earth, even as a fig tree casteth her untimely figs, when she is shaken of a mighty wind.

14 And the heaven departed as a scroll when it is rolled together; and every mountain and island were moved out of their places.

15 And the king of the earth, and the great men, and the rich men, and the chief captains, and the mighty men, and every bondman, and every free man, hid themselves in the dens and in the rocks of the mountains;

16 And said to the mountains and rocks, fall on us, and hide us from the face of him that sitteth on the throne, and from the wrath of the Lamb:

17 For the great day of his wrath is come; and who shall be able to stand?

Verse 9. With the fifth seal, John saw souls under the altar. I do not know why they were under the altar. They were killed as martyrs, so it could mean they were sacrifices. They asked how long it would be until the judgment, and the Lord answered that there were brethren and fellowservants on the earth who were still to be martyred as they had been. Just because John sees souls in heaven does not mean that they were raptured. We understand that those who are dead in Christ are in heaven. These are people who are in heaven because they died and their spirits went to heaven. Notice, too, that there are still fellow believers on earth and fellow believers are in Christ as part of the church. Pre-trib teachers would say that the brethren still on the earth are those who get saved during the Great Tribulation.

Before I get to the sixth seal, I want to go over a way to process Revelation in order to understand it. I heard a person teach that the way to understand Revelation is to look at whether John sees something is happening in heaven or on the earth. (This may be where the idea is that if you see people in heaven, it means the rapture has taken place.) This can be tricky. In Revelation 12, John says he sees a woman in heaven. As you read the rest of the chapter, you'd come to understand that the woman is on earth. We have to realize that John, during the Revelation, has been taken into heaven in the spirit, and he is in heaven seeing visions. When he saw the woman, he saw her in heaven because that's where he is. The description of what happened to the woman shows she is on the earth. It can be very difficult if this is the only way you are organizing events in Revelation. The way I see Revelation is that you have to understand that it is *not* in chronological order. We have to put it in order on the basis of the sequence of events. John right now is describing the seals and what he sees at each seal. Then he describes the next thing he sees. He cannot see everything and describe everything at once. We have to look at the sequence of events to understand what is going on and where it fits in the order of things.

Verse 12. For example, when we get to the sixth seal, there is a great earthquake. The sun becomes black as sackcloth of hair, and the moon became as blood. (We will see this again. The sun darkened, the moon becomes as blood, a great earthquake, and stars falling from heaven.) There has been much talk about "blood moons." These were eclipses of the moon that especially recently occurred on Israeli feast days. They are very significant in that this will not happen again for five hundred years. God said He set the moon in the sky not just for seasons but for signs (Gen. 1:14). Some people have related the blood moons to the prophecy of Jesus' Second Coming. Many even were hoping the rapture would occur on the last blood moon in September 2015. The scripture referring to the sun being darkened, and the moon turning as blood is occurring at the sixth seal. This is not the same event as the recent blood moons. This is not something that will happen over and over again. Jesus gives it as a sign that immediately after the Tribulation, the sun will be darkened, and the moon would not "give her light" (Matt. 24:29). What I see as a possibility is that there will be specific events such as a nuclear war creating a nuclear winter, a large meteor, or great volcanic eruption that will put so much debris into the atmosphere that it blocks the light of the sun and makes the moon look red. If you remember when Saddam Hussein caught Kuwaiti oil wells on fire, in that area, there was so much smoke that it was dark at noontime. This occurrence right before Jesus comes will be so extensive it may be over the whole earth.

Verse 14. Every mountain and island move out of their places. We will see this again later in Revelation. If mountains are going to move out of their places, and it is seen again later in Revelation, does that meant it is going to happen twice? Or should we recognize that the happening is referring to the same event when we see it again?

Verse 15. The same group of people mentioned here (kings, great men, rich men, chief captains, mighty men, bond and free) we will see at the battle of Armageddon. These will be consumed with the sword of Jesus' mouth, and the fowls of the air are called to eat of their flesh. This is the same group almost identically. But this is only the sixth seal in the sixth chapter of Revelation. The battle of Armageddon does not occur until Revelation 19. It is referring to the same event.

Verse 16. These people call on the rocks and mountains to fall on them. That makes sense since the mountains are moving out of their place. They say, "Hide us from the face of Him that sits on the throne and from the wrath of the Lamb." Why? They are going to see Him come in the clouds of heaven. They are going to see His face. It was discussed previously that every eye will see him.

Revelation 1:7

7   Behold, he cometh with clouds; and every eye shall see him, and they also which pierced him: and all kindreds of the earth shall wail because of him. Even so, Amen.

Verse 17. Then it says, "For the great day of His wrath is come." He is going to destroy them. When? At the battle of Armageddon. This will be shown further in Revelation and discussed later in this text. This passage explains that this event, that of Jesus coming to the battle of Armageddon is the *day of His wrath.* The church will not be subject to this wrath, because we have met Him in the air and put on a resurrected body.

The sixth seal is bringing us up to the event of what is known as the winepress of the wrath of God at Jesus' coming. Verse 14 says the heavens depart as a scroll. Matthew 24:27 says as the lightening shines from the east to the west so is the coming of the Son of Man.

In the book of Revelation, as we will discuss, there are seven seals, vials and seven trumpets. You will find that when we get to the sixth seal, the sixth trumpet and the sixth vial, that they are talking of the event right before the coming of Lord. With the sounding of the sixth trumpet, people are being drawn to the battle of Armageddon. It is the same way with the sixth vial. Then when we read the seventh seal, the seventh trumpet, and seventh vial, all three are showing events at Jesus' coming.

It is similar to if you are reading a book about the Civil War, and the author goes into events leading up to the south seceding. It discusses getting into the war and the battles. Then the author brings up President Lincoln for the first time maybe in the fourth chapter. He then stops, moves away from the war, and in the fifth chapter does a biography of President Lincoln. This is not in chronological order with the events of the Civil War, but the author couldn't put everything in the same place. Now that the author has brought you up to par about Lincoln, he gets back into the Civil War. You can see this in movies, especially if the director is good at it. The screen may fade away, you understand that now he is showing the adult character in his childhood and then he comes back to the present.

This may be the best way to grasp this. Think about an old movie of a pirate with his telescope, measuring about a foot and a half long. That telescope is the seven seals. Then the pirate pulls out another section. If you have three sections that get extended out, the next section is the seven trumpets and the third section is the seven vials. As you push these back in place, they all end at the same place (The sixth and seventh seal, trumpet, and vial) on the telescope.

The events shown here in the sixth seal will be seen again. Even though this is only the sixth chapter, it is referring to the last events right before Jesus' coming. Later, we will cover the scriptures in Matthew, but I want to make this point now.

Matthew 24:21, 29 – 31

21 For then shall be great tribulation, such as was not since the beginning of the world to this time, no, nor ever shall be.

29 Immediately *after* the tribulation of those days shall the sun be darkened, and the moon shall not give her light, and the stars shall fall from heaven, and the powers of the heavens shall be shaken:

30 And *then* shall appear the sign of the Son of man in heaven: and then shall all the tribes of the earth mourn, and they shall see the Son of man coming in the clouds of heaven with power and great glory.

31 And he shall send his angels with a great sound of a trumpet, and they shall *gather together* his elect from the four winds, from one end of heaven to the other.

Verse 21, says there will be Tribulation such as never was or ever shall be. This is the Great Tribulation Period. If it isn't referring to the Great Tribulation, then this one would have to be worse.

Verse 29. Immediately after the Tribulation of those days, the sun will be darkened, the moon will not give her light, and the stars shall fall (this happens in Rev. 6: 13). The powers of heaven shall be shaken. We will see these events over and over again, and they are referring to the same event right before He comes. (Revelation 6, 8, 12, 21)

Verse 30. Then shall appear the sign of the Son of Man (as the lightening shines from the east to the west) and then shall all the tribes of the earth morn. (Remember in Rev. 1:7, the kindreds of the earth wail when they see Jesus coming with clouds.) Pre-trib teachers state that Jesus coming is as a thief in the night (I Thessalonians 5:2), therefore He will sneak down to the air, meet us when we are raptured and take us to heaven. No one on the earth will see Him and will wonder where all the people have gone. More circular reasoning. First, the meaning of coming as a thief is that we do not know when He is coming, just as we would not know when a thief is coming. Jesus even says that if a man knew then a thief was coming, he would be prepared for it.

Matt 24:43

43 But know this, that if the goodman of the house had known in what watch the thief would come, he would have watched, and would not have suffered his house to be broken up.

Secondly, we are told that every eye shall see Jesus when He comes. It will be as dramatic as the lightening shining from the east to the west. Ever see a sky lit up with lightening? There is no scripture that specifically states that Jesus will come secretly at an earlier time than this Second Coming. That will only have to happen if there is a pre-trib rapture. The circular reasoning is that there is a pre-trib rapture, therefore, Jesus has to come just in the air (before the Tribulation period,) and take the church to heaven. Jesus comes in the air because the rapture is pre-trib. The rapture is pre-trib because Jesus is coming in the air. Round and round we go, yet the scriptures do not support either one. The church meets Him in the air at His coming, which we are told is immediately after the tribulation and every eye shall see Him. It reminds me of an "Andy Griffith" show in which Andy is asking questions of a man engaging in a feud. It went something like this, "Why are you shooting at them?" "Because they are Mayfields." "Well then, why are you shooting at the Mayfields?" "Because there is a feud." Why is there a feud?" "Because we are shooting at them." Or a Cary Grant Movie, "You remind me of a man" What man? "The man with the power." "What power?" "The power of Whodo." "Whodo?" "You do." "Do what?" "You remind me of a man...." This is the Cary Grant movie, The Bachelor and the Bobby-Soxer, 1947 with Shirley Temple and Myrna Loy. Another example is the Abbott and Costello baseball skit, "Who's on First." Costello tells Abbott the names of baseball players, Who, What and I Don't Know. Who is on first base, What is on second. As the skit goes on you can imagine how it progresses when Costello tells Abbott that Who's on first. Abbott asks what his name is and Costello tells him, Who, Abbott answers, I don't know and Costello says that I don't know is on third. So, Abbott asks What is the name of the man on first and Costello says, "No, What is on second." "Then who is on first?" "What is his name?"

I am being facetious, but it can help us see how circular reasoning can affect understanding. A scripture doesn't fit a doctrine, so it has to be taken another way. As I said previously, when scripture after scripture has to be explained to mean something else, then there is something wrong with the doctrine. It has been said, "This particular scripture doesn't tell us the rapture is before the tribulation, but when you put them all together, then it can be seen. The problem is that when the scriptures are "put together," they are each being explained to fit the pre-trib teaching.

Verse 31. He sends his angels with a great sound of a trumpet, and they gather together his elect from one end of heaven to the other. (Mark 13:27 says He gathers them from the uttermost part of earth to the uttermost part of heaven.) What is this? He is coming in verse 30. There is a trumpet sound and a gathering together in verse 31. This is the rapture. Notice when it says it happens—after the Tribulation. What is it doing here if there is a pre-trib rapture? Some say the elect is referring to Jews, not Christians. This is not the case. There are scriptures in the New Testament that refer to believers as the elect (Rom. 8:33, Col. 3:12, 1 Peter 1:2).

The seventh seal is addressed in later chapters in the book of Revelation and will be covered as references appear.

CHAPTER 5

The 144,000 and the Seven Trumpets

Revelation 7

1 And after these things I saw four angels standing on the four corners of the earth, holding the four winds of the earth, that the wind should not blow on the earth, nor on the sea, nor on any tree.

2 And I saw another angel ascending from the east, having the seal of the living God: and he cried with a loud voice to the four angels, to whom it was given to hurt the earth and the sea,

3 Saying, Hurt not the earth, neither the sea, nor the trees, till we have sealed the servants of our God in their foreheads.

4 And I heard the number of them which were sealed: and there were sealed an hundred and forty and four thousands of all the tribes of the children of Israel.

5- 8 of the tribe of Juda were sealed twelve thousand. Of the tribe of Reuben were sealed twelve thousand. Of the tribe of Gad were sealed twelve thousand...Aser, Nepthali, Manasses, Simeon, Levi, Issachar, Zabulon, Joseph, Benjamin.

9   After this I beheld, and, lo, a great multitude, which no man could number, of all nations, and kindreds, and people, and tongues, stood before the throne, and before the Lamb, clothed with white robes, and palms in their hands;

10 And cried with a loud voice, saying, Salvation to our God which sitteth upon the throne, and unto the Lamb.

11 And all the angels stood round about the throne, and about the elders and the four beasts, and fell before the throne on their faces, and worshipped God,

12 Saying, Amen: Blessing, and glory, and wisdom, and thanksgiving, and honour, and power, and might, be unto our God for ever and ever. Amen.

13 And one of the elders answered, saying unto me, what are these which are arrayed in white robes? And whence came they?

14 And I said unto him, Sir, thou knowest. And he said to me, these are they which came out of great tribulation, and have washed their robes, and made them white in the blood of the Lamb.

15 Therefore are they before the throne of God, and serve him day and night in his temple: and he that sitteth on the throne shall dwell among them.

16 They shall hunger no more, neither thirst anymore; neither shall the sun light on them, nor any heat.

17 For the Lamb which is in the midst of the throne shall feed them, and shall lead them

unto living fountains of waters: and God shall
wipe away all tears from their eyes.

Verses 1–2. The angels are told not to hurt the earth, the sea, or
the trees until the servants of God are sealed. This demonstrates
people being kept during the tribulation. We will soon see that the
sea will turn as blood and one-third of creatures in the sea will die,
then later all will die. The trees and the grass will be burnt.

Verse 3. As the "mark of the beast" is presented as a mark in the
hand or forehead, God has a seal He puts in the forehead. Believers
are told that we are sealed by the Holy Spirit (Eph. 1:13) unto the
day of redemption. God marks His own. Ezekiel sees a man with an
inkhorn (ink well) in a vision. This man is told to mark those that
were crying because of sin. Those that had the mark were not killed.

Ezekiel 9: 3 – 6

3   ... And he called to the man clothed with linen,
     which had the writer's inkhorn by his side;

4   And the Lord said unto him, Go through
     the midst of the city, through the midst of
     Jerusalem, and set a mark upon the foreheads
     of the men that sigh and that cry for all
     the abominations that be done in the midst
     thereof.

5   And to the others he said in mine hearing, Go
     ye after him through the city, and smite: let
     not your eye spare, neither have ye pity:

6   Slay utterly old and young, both maids, and
     little children, and women: but come not near
     any man upon whom is the mark; and begin at
     my sanctuary. Then they began at the ancient
     men which were before the house.

Verses 5–8. There are 144,000 sealed: Twelve thousand from
twelve tribes of Israel. Notice the multiple of twelve, which is the
number for government in the scripture. When we discuss the New
Jerusalem later, we will see the 144,000 again as a measurement. It

is a city foursquare, 12,000 by 12,000 furlongs. The tribes of Israel are the sons of Jacob whose name was changed to Israel. Whenever the land was divided, it didn't go to the exact twelve sons of Israel. Joseph (the one who was sold by his brothers to Egypt and saved his family when they came to Egypt for food) was given the double portion in that his two children—Ephraim and Manasseh—were given a share of land. This would have made thirteen, but the tribe of Levi did not get a specific share of land. They were the priestly tribe and were given parts of the other land for their inheritance. In this group of twelve in Revelation, for some reason, Dan is not mentioned. Some have said he isn't here because a calf was erected for worship in Dan. The problem with that rationale is that all of the other tribes had groves (poles to worship the goddess Asherah) and altars of Baal. I do not know why Dan is left out. Instead of Ephraim and Manasseh (the sons of Joseph), it says Joseph and Manasseh and leaves off Ephraim.

I am not satisfied with explanations I have heard about this 144,000, who they are, and why there are sealed. We will read in a later chapter that these are the redeemed from the earth and the firstfruits (meaning first harvest). Some say there will be 12,000 of each of the tribes of Israel who will get saved and sealed and preach the gospel during the Great Tribulation. I just do not think that God is so arbitrary. Why 12,000 exactly? What if there are more in one tribe? Will God say, "Too bad, I can only pick 12,000 to be sealed"? If these are all the redeemed, why is it specifically only the tribes of Israel? I just think there is something more here than what I understand. I just do not know what it is, yet. I have some puzzle pieces such as the multiple of twelve and the connection to the dimensions of the New Jerusalem. I just haven't finished the puzzle.

Verse 14. Robes were "made white in the blood of the Lamb". Having worked in white as a nurse (few wear white anymore), I know how hard it is to get blood out of a white uniform. I know the symbolism of the blood of Jesus cleansing sin. Only Jesus' blood could make anything white.

Verses 9–17. This section could have been a different chapter. We will read in Rev. 21 that this is how things are described on the new earth after the millennial reign and the Great White Throne Judgment. The first eight verses of this chapter (Rev. 7) are addressing the twelve tribes of Israel being sealed to protect them. Perhaps this is emphasizing that whether you get sealed as part of the 144,000 or you are sealed in Christ, your final end will be one of glorious victory.

Revelation 8

1 And when he had opened the seventh seal, there was silence in heaven about the space of half an hour.

2 And I saw the seven angels which stood before God; and to them were given seven trumpets.

3 And another angel came and stood at the altar, having a golden censer; and there was given unto him much incense, that he should offer it with the prayers of all saints upon the golden altar which was before the throne.

4 And the smoke of the incense, which came with the prayers of the saints, ascended up before God out of the angel's hand.

5 And the angel took the censer, and filled it with fire of the altar, and cast it into the earth: and there were voices, and thunderings, and lightnings, and an earthquake.

6 And the seven angels which had the seven trumpets prepared themselves to sound.

7 The first angel sounded, and there followed hail and fire mingled with blood, and they were cast upon the earth: and the third of trees was burnt up, and all green grass was burnt up.

8 And the second angel sounded, and as it were a great mountain burning with fire was cast into the sea: and the third part of the sea became blood;

9   And the third part of the creatures which were in the sea, and had life, died; and the third part of the ships were destroyed.

10 And the third angel sounded, and there fell a great star from heaven, burning as it were a lamp, and it fell upon the third part of the rivers, and upon the fountains of waters;

11 And the name of the star is called Wormwood: and the third part of the waters became wormwood; and many men died of the waters, because they were made bitter.

12 And the fourth angel sounded, and the third part of the sun was smitten, and the third part of the moon, and the third part of the stars; so as the third part of them was darkened, and the day shone not for a third part of it, and the night likewise.

13 And I beheld, and heard an angel flying through the midst of heaven, saying with a loud voice, Woe, woe, woe, to the inhabiters of the earth by reason of the other voices of the trumpet of the three angels, which are yet to sound!

Verse 1. We are at the end of the closed telescope—the seventh seal—where the coming of the Lord is. It states that when he opens the seventh seal, there is silence in heaven about the space of half an hour. Why silence in heaven, I am not sure. We read that worship is going on continuously around the throne and now silence. It could be that when Jesus comes, the event is so dramatic that all of heaven is silent to take notice. Why a half hour? I heard one idea that a day is a year, and when you calculate a half hour, it will be about a week, so it will take Jesus a week to get from heaven to earth. Why would it take Jesus a week to get here? Just a thought would bring Him here instantly. I heard recently that the space of half an hour or an hour is an idiom that meant a short while. This is comparable to when we say, "Just a second," or "In a minute." This explanation seems more reasonable.

Verse 2. Now the telescope is opened up, and John will describe what he sees when the trumpets sound. Angels are given trumpets. He sees the prayers of saints as incense mingled with fire and thrown to the earth. Our prayers have impact.

Verse 5. As the censor is thrown to the earth, there were voices, lightning, thunder, and an earthquake.

Verse 6. The trumpets prepare to sound. Does one sound and all the events John sees occur before the next trumpet sounds? Or is it that the trumpets sound, one after the other, but John can only describe what he sees with each trumpet one at a time?

Verse 7. The first trumpet sounds, and there follows hail and fire mingled with blood, a third of trees is burnt up and all green grass.

Exodus 9: 23 – 25

23 And Moses stretched forth his rod toward heaven: and the Lord sent thunder and hail, and the fire ran along upon the ground; and the Lord rained hail upon the land of Egypt.

24 So there was hail, and fire mingled with the hail, very grievous, such as there was none like it in all the land of Egypt since it became a nation.

25 And the hail smote throughout all the land of Egypt all that was in the field, both man and beast;

This occurred when the plagues were hitting Egypt. Moses is dealing with Pharaoh to let the children of Israel go. This passage doesn't mention blood, but there was bloodshed because of the hail. I don't know how this can happen. How would you have hail and fire? Is the fire associated with a huge amount of lightning or could this occur with another geographic disaster as a volcanic eruption? If the fire is lightning, why doesn't this say lightning?

Verses 8–9. The second trumpet sounds, and there is a great mountain burning with fire cast into the sea, a third of the sea becomes blood, and a third of the creatures in the sea die, and a third of ships were destroyed. Does the blood mean death since a third part of the sea becomes blood, and it is a third part of the creatures that die, or does the sea look blood red? I have seen documentaries regarding red tides due to an algae creating a toxin poisonous to living organisms.

A great mountain burning with fire could be a volcano on an island that then falls into the sea. I have heard that there are islands with fault lines in which that could happen. In this case, it would create a great tsunami. I heard someone describe a mountain burning with fire as the way a mushroom cloud from a nuclear bomb would have looked to John, like what happened in Nagasaki and Hiroshima during WWII. A problem with this idea is that the mushroom clouds went up. They did not appear to be "cast in the sea." The invisible radiated cloud eventually dropped radiation to the earth as it followed air currents, but this is not the same as a mountain seen as being "cast in the sea." There are many ideas; it may be we will only recognize what John is seeing when it actually happens. I have heard that of the number of ships in WWII that there were a third of them destroyed.[3]

Verses 10–11. The third trumpet sounds, and a star from heaven burns as a lamp. It falls on a third of the rivers and waters, and the name of the star is Wormwood (which means bitter). A third part of the waters become bitter, and many die because of the bitter water. A star falling from heaven burning as a lamp could be a meteorite, but how would it affect a third of rivers and waters unless it is a meteor shower? In addition, how would it make the waters bitter?

Russians recognize the word *Wormwood* because in Russian, the word Chernobyl is translated Wormwood. If you remember in 1986, a nuclear power plant Chernobyl had a meltdown. Some of the men who were sent to Chernobyl to clean up were killed instantly. After it was known that there was severe radiation, men were put in suits with masks and told they could only spend a very short time throwing debris off the roof and them come away. A remote vehicle that was sent to do the job malfunctioned because of the high radiation count. There was an explosion up into the sky, and radioactivity was blown into the air then fell back down, following air currents throughout Europe. Rain would have dropped the radiation down into rivers. Way up in Scandinavia, farmers had to kill thousands of caribou because they had been contaminated by the radiation. That event fits this very closely. The way I looked at this years ago is that perhaps the effect would be in greater evidence at the time of the Great Tribulation. Some that worked in the area immediately died, but depending upon the amount or exposure, the strength, and distance from exposure, cancers and sickness could take twenty or thirty years to emerge. I remember watching a documentary about ten years later called, *The Children of Chernobyl,* in which teenagers (who would have been little when the melt down occurred) in Kiev, which is about fifty miles away, were presenting to doctors with no hair anywhere on their body. The doctors wouldn't say for sure that it was earlier radiation exposure. But at the time of the meltdown, no one was warned, and children would have been out playing and got exposed. It also was stated that the waste, such as pieces of cement that will be contaminated for a long time, was just put into waste dumps in the area. It was said that eventually, the radiation would get into the ground water, into the Black Sea, then into the ocean.

Since then, there was the explosion in a nuclear power plant after the tsunami hit Japan. It may be that the effects of these will show up during the Great Tribulation. It could be that Chernobyl is a harbinger of what will occur. I wonder if we could get rosters of employees at nuclear power plants, if we would recognize possible saboteurs. In addition, nuclear power plants need water. Some have been built on fault lines. Earthquakes could cause trouble as was the case in Japan. Have you heard anything about the amount of radiation that was released from that instance? It seems that the information is being kept from us. The jet stream could have taken that radiation across America. We just don't know how contaminated (bitter) the waters are becoming. I just heard recently about a fire close to nuclear waste. How secure is all the radioactive waste from all the years that all the nuclear power plants have been operating?

Verse 12. The fourth angel sounds, and a third part of the sun, moon, and stars are darkened, and the light doesn't shine for a third part of the day and the night. I do not know how this occurs. How a third part of the sun can be darkened, and how it would affect a third part of a day? Perhaps a scientist could come up with an idea as to what John is describing. Does John mean a third part of the earth will only be dark for a third part of the day? How long will it last. Just a day or a period of time? This may just be another thing that we won't know for sure what it is until we see it.

Verse 13. An angel describes the last three trumpets as woes. The first woe will be the fifth trumpet. I have heard recently from a source (one from which I have gained insight) that says these trumpets may have started back at WWI and the incident of Chernobyl is actually the third angel sounding in 1986.[3] I had never thought about the fact that there isn't anything in Revelation that says the trumpets couldn't start until the Great Tribulation. I just assumed this to be the case. I have questions, however, about things that do not seem to fit. I wonder that since the two prophets in Revelation 11:3 do not start their ministry until the three and a half year time that the angels won't sound until this time.

Revelation 9:1 – 12

1   And the fifth angel sounded, and I saw a star fall from heaven unto the earth: and to him was given the key of the bottomless pit.

2   And he opened the bottomless pit; and there arose a smoke out of the pit, as the smoke of a great furnace; and the sun and the air were darkened by reason of the smoke of the pit.

3   And there came out of the smoke locusts upon the earth: and unto them was given power, as the scorpions of the earth have power.

4   And it was commanded them that they should not hurt the grass of the earth neither any green thing, neither any tree; but only those

men which have not the seal of God in their foreheads.

5 And to them it was given that they should not kill them, but that they should be tormented five months: and their torment was as the torment of a scorpion, when he striketh a man.

6 And in those days shall men seek death, and shall not find it; and shall desire to die, and death shall flee from them.

7 And the shapes of the locusts were like unto horses prepared unto battle; and on their heads were as it were crowns like gold, and their faces were as the faces of men.

8 And they had hair as the hair of women, and their teeth were as the teeth of lions.

9 And they had breastplates, as it were breastplates of iron; and the sound of their wings was as the sound of chariots of many horses running to battle.

10 And they had tails like unto scorpions, and there were stings in their tails: and their power was to hurt men five months.

11 And they had a king over them, which is the angel of the bottomless pit, whose name in the Hebrew tongue is Abaddon, but in the Greek tongue hath his name Apollyon.

12 One woe is past; and, behold, there come two woes more hereafter.

Verses 1–2. The fifth angel sounds. A star could be a star (which isn't likely. An actual star, like our sun would bring total destruction.) It could be something that looks like a star (such as a meteor or missile) or an angel. This star falls from heaven and opens the bottomless pit from which arises a great smoke, and the sun and air are darkened. Could this be oil wells on fire, or missile silos releasing nuclear bombs?

Verse 3. Locusts come out of the smoke and were given power as scorpions. The locust are described in verses 7–9 as horses prepared to battle with crowns of gold, faces of men, and hair as women. Their teeth as lions, breastplates of iron, and wings the sound of chariots of many horses running to battle. Can you think of technology today that would sound like chariots of horses running to battle? A helicopter comes to mind. I was thinking on this that I had only seen black helicopters, so why crowns of gold? Then I saw a scene on television of a helicopter in Iraq that was sandy colored. I thought, *there is the crown of gold.* You can see faces of men through the windshield. I also wondered about the hair as a woman, and I saw a helicopter that between the chopper and the blade, there was a section that looked like a bun like a woman would wear, if her hair were up. Helicopters have guns; they could shoot bullets or possibly chemical or biological substances.

Verses 5–10. The locusts torment for five months. People would seek death or desire to die, but death would flee from them. I wondered how a person could desire to die but not be able to kill themselves, and I thought of shows in which a paralyzed person begged someone else to kill them. Perhaps soon (if there isn't already), there will be a type of nerve gas that creates a painful paralysis that lasts five months. Those not affected could take care of the ones exposed until five months later when the effects wear off. Just some thoughts.

Verse 12. One has said that the word Abaddon means destroyer, and Saddam means destroyer. Interesting thought since Saddam Hussein blew up many oil wells causing the smoke to darken the air and sun. I just do not remember anything occurring during Desert Shield that caused torment for five months.

I hope alternative solutions do no not bother you. You may have heard different ones. I said that I have more questions than answers. I may lean toward one answer over another, but I will not insist it is the right answer when it is only conjecture. If ours is not the generation that brings on the coming of the Lord, there may be technological advances in the future that will seem more reasonable.

Revelation 9:13 – 21

13 And the sixth angel sounded, and I heard a voice from the four horns of the golden altar which is before God,

14 Saying to the sixth angel which had the trumpet, Loose the four angels which are bound in the great river Euphrates.

15 And the four angels were loosed, which were prepared for an hour, and a day, and a month, and a year, for to slay the third part of men.

16 And the number of the army of the horsemen were two hundred thousand thousand: and I heard the number of them.

17 And thus I saw the horses in the vision, and them that sat on them, having breastplates of fire, and of jacinth, and brimstone: and the heads of the horses were as the heads of lions; and out of their mouths issued fire and smoke and brimstone.

18 By these three was the third part of men killed, by the fire, and by the smoke, and by the brimstone, which issued out of their mouths.

19 For their power is in their mouth, and in their tails: for their tails were like unto serpents, and had heads, and with them they do hurt.

20 And the rest of the men which were not killed by these plagues yet repented not of the works of their hands, that they should not worship devils, and idols of gold, and silver, and brass, and stone, and of wood: which neither can see, nor hear, nor walk:

21 Neither repented they of their murders, nor of
their sorceries, nor of their fornication, nor of
their thefts.

Verses 13–15. The sixth angel sounds. It mentions the river
Euphrates. The sixth vial refers to the Euphrates River drying up.
Turkey has built a dam on the Euphrates River and could actually
dry up the river.

Verse 16. An army of two hundred million will come from east of
the Euphrates River. Some have suggested China. China has enough
of a population to have an army that large and we are seeing China
climb in technological and economic advances.

Verses 17–19. John sees horses and describes them as having
breastplates of fire and brimstone (or Sulphur). The heads are as
lions, and out of their mouths issued fire and brimstone. A third
of men are killed. Power is in their mouth and tails. I can think of
army tanks, men walking along them in biological suits with gas
masks, with the big missile type bazookas. I heard a documentary
suggesting that John may be seeing artificial intelligence in play. It
was stated that there are in existence today, robots that could be
used in battle instead of using humans. The suggestion is that this
artificial intelligence could decide that humans are not necessary
and will come against mankind. This is farfetched to me, especially
when the scriptures teach that the beast will fight against Israel and
when Jesus returns and ends the battle of Armageddon, it is human
beings that die and real blood that is shed.

Verses 20–21. In all the trouble, people still don't repent.

Revelation 10

1 And I saw another mighty angel come down
from heaven, clothed with a cloud: and a
rainbow was upon his head, and his face was
as it were the sun, and his feet as pillars of
fire:

2 And he had in his hand a little book open:
and he set his right foot upon the sea, and his

left foot on the earth, 3 And cried with a loud voice, as when a lion roareth: and when he had cried, seven thunder suttered their voices.

4 And when the seven thunders had uttered their voices, I was about to write: and I heard a voice from heaven saying unto me, Seal up those things which the seven thunders uttered, and write them not.

5 And the angel which I saw stand upon the sea and upon the earth lifted up his hand to heaven,

6 And sware by him that liveth for ever and ever, who created heaven, and the things that therein are, and the earth, and the things that therein are, and the sea and the things which are therein, that there should be time no longer:

7 But in the days of the voice of the seventh angel, when he shall begin to sound, the mystery of God should be finished, as he hath declared to his servants the prophets.

8 And the voice which I heard from heaven spake unto me again, and said, Go and take the little book which is open in the hand of the angel which standeth upon the sea and upon the earth.

9 And I went unto the angel, and said unto him, Give me the little book. And he said unto me, Take it, and eat it up; and it shall make thy belly bitter, but it shall be in thy mouth sweet as honey.

10 And I took the little book out of the angel's hand, and ate it up; and it was in my mouth sweet as honey: and as soon as I had eaten it, my belly was bitter.

11 And he said unto me, Thou must prophesy again before many peoples, and nations, and tongues, and kings.

Verses 1–4. Mentions a mighty angel that has a book, thunders utter their voice, and John is told to seal the things up and not write them. Daniel was told not to reveal words of a book and that it would be revealed at the time of the end.

Daniel 12:4, 9

4   But thou, O Daniel, shut up the words, and seal the book, to the time of the end: many shall run to and fro, and knowledge shall be increased.

9   And he said, Go thy way, Daniel: for the words are closed up and sealed till the time of the end.

THE MYSTERY OF GOD IS FINISHED

Verse 7. In Chapter 11, it mentions the seventh trumpet again and says that *now* the kingdoms of the earth have become the kingdoms of Jesus, so we know that Jesus has come and will set up His rule and reign. This says, "In the days of the voice of the seventh angel . . . the mystery of God should be finished." I had thought of what this mystery is. Then recently, I heard another source use the same example.[3] There are different mysteries of God. Jesus said to his disciples that it was given to them to know the mysteries of the Kingdom, (Matt. 13:11). One mystery that comes to mind is where Paul speaks of "Christ in you the hope of glory" (Col. 1:27). A mystery that is specifically mentioned in regards to the endtime is:

I Corinthians 15: 51 – 52

51 Behold, I shew you a mystery; We shall not all sleep, but we shall all be changed,

52 In a moment, in the twinkling of an eye, at the last trump: for the trumpet shall sound, and

the dead shall be raised incorruptible, and we
shall be changed.

This is referring to the rapture. When the seventh angel sounds the seventh trumpet, the mystery of God is finished. This certainly fits the scripture referring to a mystery that the dead being raised and changed occurs at the last trumpet.

Verses 9–11. John is then told to eat the book, and it would be sweet in his mouth but bitter or sour in his stomach. This same thing happened to Ezekiel (Ezek. 3:2–3).

CHAPTER 6

Prophetic Judgment and Protection

Revelation 11: 1 – 4

1 And there was given me a reed like unto a rod: and the angel stood, saying, Rise, and measure the temple of God, and the altar, and them that worship therein.

2 But the court which is without the temple leave out, and measure it not; for it is given unto the Gentiles: and the holy city shall they tread under foot forty and two months.

3 And I will give power unto my two witnesses, and they shall prophesy a thousand two hundred and threescore days, clothed in sackcloth.

4 These are the two olive trees, and the two candlesticks standing before the God of the earth.

Verses 1 – 2. The temple of God is measured. I have heard that measuring the temple occurs before judgment. I don't have an opinion on that. Verse 2 seems to imply that the temple is on the earth in Jerusalem. This may mean that a temple has to be built. I mentioned previously that this temple could be built quickly. Forty-two months is three and a half years.

THE TWO WITNESSES

Verse 3. This speaks of two witnesses who prophesy. They are prophets who prophesy for three and a half years.

Verse 4. Two olive trees and two candlesticks are standing before God. Candlesticks and olive trees are mentioned in Zechariah.

Zechariah 4: 1 – 6, 10 – 14

1   And the angel that talked with me came again, and waked me, as a man that is wakened out of his sleep,

2   And said unto me, What seest thou? And I said, I have looked, and behold a candlestick all of gold, with a bowl upon the top of it, and his seven lamps thereon, and seven pipes to the seven lamps, which are upon the top thereof:

3   And two olive trees by it, one upon the right side of the bowl, and the other upon the left side thereof.

4   So I answered and spake to the angel that talked with me, saying, What are these, my lord?

5   Then the angel that talked with me answered and said unto me, Knowest thou not what these be? And I said, No, my lord.

6   Then he answered and spake unto me, saying, This is the word of the Lord unto Zerubbabel, saying, Not by might, nor by power, but by my spirit, saith the Lord of hosts.

10 For who hath despised the day of small things? for they shall rejoice, and shall see the plummet in the hand of Zerubbabel with those seven; they are the eyes of the Lord, which run to and fro through the whole earth.

11 Then answered I, and said unto him, What are these olive trees upon the right side of the candlestick and upon the left side thereof?

12 And I answered again, and said unto him, What be these two olive branches which through the golden pipes empty the golden oil out of themselves?

13 And he answered me and said, Knowest thou not what these be? And I said, No, my lord.

14 Then said he, These are the two anointed ones, that stand by the Lord of the whole earth.

Verses 1–3. Zechariah is shown a vision and sees a candlestick. Notice the seven lamps (addressed previously in Revelation as the seven Spirits of God). In verse 3, he then sees two olive trees. Verse 12 says the two olive branches empty oil, which would keep the lamp lit. Normally, olives have to be crushed to get the oil, but here, it just says the branches feed oil to the candlesticks.

Verses 5–6. In verse 6 after Zechariah asks what these things were, he was told, "Not by might, nor by power, but by my spirit." (Verse 9.) The menorah, which has seven lamps and the oil that keeps them lit may be a type and shadow of the Spirit of God (the Holy Spirit) (Heb. 8:5). This aligns with the reference to the "seven spirits of God" which was previously discussed.

Verses 12–14. It was told to Zechariah that the two olive branches are the two anointed ones that stand by the Lord. This still doesn't help me understand all of this about the two anointed ones. I heard that in the days of Zechariah, the two that would be anointed would be the king and the priest. I would not know what the connection would be to the two witnesses. One group that agrees with the idea that a day is a year (1260 days are years) says this time frame started when Constantine established the Catholic Church and ended with the French Revolution. In the French Revolution, fires were built to burn all Bibles. This, to them, means that the two witnesses are the Old and New Testament of the Bible. In the next chapter, we will see that the two prophets are killed, lie in the streets for three and a half days, then get resurrected and ascend into a cloud. How can the Old and New Testament get resurrected? As previously stated, that by knowing scripture, we can recognize immediately when a teaching is farfetched and cannot be correct. Wouldn't it be something though, if the idea that the 1260 days is actually years that haven't started yet? Imagine a Great Tribulation period lasting over twelve hundred years. Another idea is that the candlestick is the church as in Revelation 3 and the olive tree is Israel. I can see the analogy, but how can all the church and Israel be killed in Jerusalem and all lie in the street?

Revelation 11: 5 – 12

5   And if any man will hurt them, fire proceedeth out of their mouth, and devoureth their enemies: and if any man will hurt them, he must in this manner be killed.

6   These have power to shut heaven, that it rain not in the days of their prophecy: and have power over waters to turn them to blood, and to smite the earth with all plagues, as often as they will.

7   And when they shall have finished their testimony, the beast that ascendeth out of the bottomless pit shall make war against them, and shall overcome them, and kill them.

8   And their dead bodies shall lie in the street of the great city, which spiritually is called Sodom and Egypt, where also our Lord was crucified.

9   And they of the people and kindreds and tongues and nations shall see their dead bodies three days and an half, and shall not suffer their dead bodies to be put in graves.

10 And they that dwell upon the earth shall rejoice over them, and make merry, and shall send gifts one to another; because these two

prophets tormented them that dwelt on the
earth.

11 And after three days and an half the Spirit
of life from God entered into them, and they
stood upon their feet; and great fear fell upon
them which saw them.

12 And they heard a great voice from heaven
saying unto them, Come up hither. And they
ascended up to heaven in a cloud; and their
enemies beheld them.

Verses 5–6. It is still addressing the two prophets. Fire proceeds
out of their mouth. They have power to kill any who would hurt
them. They can shut up heaven so that there is no rain, can turn
water to blood, and speak plagues.

With the trumpet sounding and later we will see the same with
the vials, water was turned to blood. These prophets seem to be
prophesying what the trumpets are going to do. Just as Moses spoke
of the plagues in Egypt before they occurred, as the angels release
the plagues, the two witnesses prophecy them to happen.

Amos 3:7

7 Surely the Lord God will do nothing, but he
revealeth his secret unto his servants the
prophets.

Verses 7–8. At first, the prophets can protect themselves from
harm, but when their testimony is finished after the three and a half
years, the beast (which we will later see is the Antichrist) will kill
them and leave their bodies in the street of Jerusalem (where our
Lord was crucified).

Verse 9. People will rejoice, make merry, and send gifts. This
occurs today. After 9/11, people in Pakistan rejoiced and handed out
gifts. The prophets will be blamed for people being tormented.

Verses 11–12. After three and a half days, they come to life and ascend up into a cloud. This looks like a resurrection. Let's look at the timing of this resurrection.

Revelation 11: 13 – 19

13 And the same hour was there a great earthquake, and the tenth part of the city fell, and in the earthquake were slain of men seven thousand: and the remnant were affrighted, and gave glory to the God of heaven.

14 The second woe is past; and, behold, the third woe cometh quickly.

15 And the seventh angel sounded; and there were great voices in heaven, saying, The kingdoms of this world are become the kingdoms of our Lord, and of his Christ; and he shall reign for ever and ever.

16 And the four and twenty elders, which sat before God on their seats, fell upon their faces, and worshipped God,

17 Saying, We give thee thanks, O Lord God Almighty, which art, and wast, and art to come; because thou hast taken to thee thy great power, and hast reigned.

18 And the nations were angry, and thy wrath is come, and the time of the dead, that they should be judged, and that thou shouldest give reward unto thy servants the prophets, and to the saints, and them that fear thy name, small and great; and shouldest destroy them which destroy the earth.

19 And the temple of God was opened in heaven, and there was seen in his temple the ark of his testament: and there were lightnings, and voices, and thunderings, and an earthquake, and great hail.

Verses 13–17. Notice what happens when the two witnesses ascend. At the same hour is a great earthquake, the tenth part of the city falls. (Verse 19 says there is lightning, thundering, earthquake, and great hail.) The second woe is past (the sixth trumpet), and the third woe comes quickly (the seventh trumpet). What occurs at the seventh trumpet? The coming of the Lord. Verse 15 confirms this: It says that the kingdoms of the world have become the kingdoms of our Lord.

Verse 18. The twenty-four elders say that the nations were angry, and "thy wrath is come." Now the wrath is come? This is the coming of the Lord. How is the wrath just now coming? The reason it is now, is because this is referring to the winepress of the wrath of God at Jesus' coming at the battle of Armageddon. Believers have been raptured and are with Jesus, along with the two witnesses and are not appointed to this wrath. If we are alive and remain unto this point, we have been kept during the Great Tribulation. Some will read about the two witnesses being resurrected and claim it is another separate resurrection, but it isn't. There is only one rapture and resurrection of the dead in Christ. I show again the scripture that speaks of the order of resurrection and receiving a resurrected body, that Jesus is the firstfruits, then we at His coming.

I Corinthians 15:23

23 But every man in his own order: Christ the
first fruits; afterward they that are Christ's at
his coming.

We will see later in Revelation that the resurrection of the dead in Christ at the time of the coming of the Lord is the referred to as the first resurrection. If it is the first, there is none before it. There cannot be a bunch of resurrections in the first resurrection because it is called the first. If there were a bunch before it, it wouldn't be the first.

It says the two prophets lie in the street for three and a half days. If we witness their death, then we will know when they will be resurrected. Jesus said we wouldn't know the day and the hour. But at this point, it may be that in all the turmoil and commotion, we will be looking up while others are asking for the rocks and mountains to fall on them because we know our redemption draws nigh.

Zechariah 14: 2 – 4

2   For I will gather all nations against Jerusalem to battle; and the city shall be taken,

3   Then shall the Lord go forth, and fight against those nations, as when he fought in the day of battle.

4   And his feet shall stand in that day upon the mount of Olives, which is before Jerusalem on the east, and the mount of Olives shall cleave in the midst thereof toward the east and toward the west, and there shall be a very great valley; and half of the mountain shall remove toward the north, and half of it toward the south.

Verse 4. This speaks to Jesus' coming. He lands on Mt. Olives, and the mountain splits in a great earthquake. There are various teachings as to the identity of the two witnesses. Some have said they are Moses and Elijah because these appeared with Jesus at the transfiguration (Matt. 17:2–3). Moses turned water to blood, and Elijah shut up the heavens. Some have said they could have the spirit of Moses and Elijah. (Meaning they would function with the same anointing, or calling.) John the Baptist had the same anointing as Elijah. Others have said this is Elijah and Enoch because these never died, and they will need to experience death. Any of these are possible although I do not know why Enoch and Elijah could not just put on a resurrected body at the same time as those who are in the rapture.

In any case, we know that there will be two prophetic voices that prophesy these things. As the angels release them, God has someone prophesying them during the three and a half years of the Great Tribulation.

Revelation 12

1   And there appeared a great wonder in heaven;
     a woman clothed with the sun, and the moon
     under her feet, and upon her head a crown of
     twelve stars:

2   And she being with child cried, travailing in
     birth, and pained to be delivered.

3   And there appeared another wonder in
     heaven; and behold a great red dragon, having
     seven heads and ten horns, and seven crowns
     upon his heads.

4   And his tail drew the third part of the stars of
     heaven, and did cast them to the earth: and
     the dragon stood before the woman which
     was ready to be delivered, for to devour her
     child as soon as it was born.

5   And she brought forth a man child, who was
     to rule all nations with a rod of iron: and her
     child was caught up unto God, and to his
     throne.

6   And the woman fled into the wilderness,
     where she hath a place prepared of God, that
     they should feed her there a thousand two
     hundred and threescore days.

7   And there was war in heaven: Michael and
     his angels fought against the dragon; and the
     dragon fought and his angels,

8   And prevailed not; neither was their place
     found any more in heaven.

9   And the great dragon was cast out, that old
     serpent, called the Devil, and Satan, which
     deceiveth the whole world: he was cast out
     into the earth, and his angels were cast out
     with him.

10 And I heard a loud voice saying in heaven, Now is come salvation, and strength, and the kingdom of our God, and the power of his Christ: for the accuser of our brethren is cast down, which accused them before our God day and night.

11 And they overcame him by the blood of the Lamb, and by the word of their testimony; and they loved not their lives unto the death.

12 Therefore rejoice, ye heavens, and ye that dwell in them. Woe to the inhabiters of the earth and of the sea! for the devil is come down unto you, having great wrath, because he knoweth that he hath but a short time.

13 And when the dragon saw that he was cast unto the earth, he persecuted the woman which brought forth the man child.

14 And to the woman were given two wings of a great eagle, that she might fly into the wilderness, into her place, where she is nourished for a time, and times, and half a time, from the face of the serpent.

15 And the serpent cast out of his mouth water as a flood after the woman, that he might cause her to be carried away of the flood.

16 And the earth helped the woman, and the earth opened her mouth, and swallowed up the flood which the dragon cast out of his mouth.

17 And the dragon was wroth with the woman, and went to make war with the remnant of her seed, which keep the commandments of God, and have the testimony of Jesus Christ.

THE WOMAN CLOTHED WITH THE SUN

This seems like a chapter that is just interjected right here. John sees a great wonder, a woman clothed with the sun, the moon under her feet, and she has a crown with twelve stars. She delivers a man child. The dragon (Satan) tries to devour her child. The child is caught up to the throne. The woman is kept in a wilderness place that was prepared for her where she is protected for the three and a half years. The dragon is cast to the earth along with angels that followed him (a third part of the stars). Satan makes war with her seed, which have the testimony of Jesus.

Verse 1. Who is the woman? Some have said she is Mary because she brought forth Jesus. This explanation falls short because I know of no time that Mary had to be taken to a wilderness for three and a half years. One that makes the most sense to me is that the woman is Israel. The twelve stars are the twelve tribes of Israel. Jesus comes from the nation of Israel.[3] We know the man child is Jesus because verse 5 says he is to rule with a rod of iron and he is caught up to the throne. Israel has been given a place in the wilderness with the new nation. Israel has blossomed since Israel became a nation in 1948. It was more of a desert place prior to this. This passage is showing that Israel will be kept during these three and a half years of Great Tribulation. Even though satanic influences surrounding Israel want her wiped off the map, it will not happen. Jesus will return to Jerusalem and set up His rule and reign from there.

A more "spiritualized" idea of the woman is that she is believers in the church (a people among a people) that "brought forth a man child" meaning have put on the "fullness of the stature of Jesus Christ." Believers will also rule and reign with a rod of iron with Jesus. These believers can be caught up to the throne spiritually. This is very "far out there", and the more simplistic explanation of the woman being Israel makes more sense. Again, as always, there may be more to this passage, but I feel the point that the woman is Israel is likely the case.

Verse 4. Some have said that this war in heaven happened in the past in which Satan made war and took a third of the angels with him to earth. John was told in Revelation 4 that he would be shown things in the future.

Verse 10 implies that Satan still has access to the throne and is our accuser. He finally loses this access and is kicked out permanently. Satan is our accuser; Jesus is our advocate.

Verse 11. This is a popular scripture because it can apply to believers showing that we overcome with the blood of the lamb and the word of our testimony. There is no situation in our lives in which we cannot apply the blood of Jesus and overcome by speaking the Word into the situation. Whether it is forgiveness of sin, deliverance from strongholds, or sickness, we can be overcomers.

Verse 17. Because Satan sees that Israel is protected, he then goes after Christians (those who have the testimony of Jesus Christ).

CHAPTER 7

Persecution and Harvest

Revelation 13: 1 – 9

1   And I stood upon the sand of the sea, and saw a beast rise up out of the sea, having seven heads and ten horns, and upon his horns ten crowns, and upon his heads the name of blasphemy.

2   And the beast which I saw was like unto a leopard, and his feet were as the feet of a bear, and his mouth as the mouth of a lion: and the dragon gave him his power, and his seat, and great authority.

3   And I saw one of his heads as it were wounded to death; and his deadly wound was healed: and all the world wondered after the beast.

4   And they worshipped the dragon which gave power unto the beast: and they worshipped the beast, saying, Who is like unto the beast? who is able to make war with him?

5   And there was given unto him a mouth speaking great things and blasphemies; and power was given unto him to continue forty and two months.

6   And he opened his mouth in blasphemy against God, to blaspheme his name, and his tabernacle, and them that dwell in heaven.

7   And it was given unto him to make war with the saints, and to overcome them: and power was given him over kindreds, and tongues, and nations.

8   And all that dwell upon the earth shall worship him, whose names are not written in the book of life of the Lamb slain from the foundation of the world.

9   If any man have an ear, let him hear.

THE BEAST AND HIS MARK

Verses 1 – 2. John sees a beast with seven heads and ten horns. The beast can refer to a particular person whom we call the Antichrist, and it can refer to the system or kingdom the beast will rule. The beast is like unto a leopard. The beast will rule over nations that exist at the time. One source refers to nations with which the animals are associated. Germany is referred to as a leopard. Russia (even in magazine articles) is known as a bear, and the lion is Great Britain.[3] If this is so, then these nations present now will exist during the three and a half year period and will be part of the beast system. Another source takes a middle-east perspective instead of a western perspective and says that the leopard is Greece. The lion is Babylon (Iraq and Arabia) and the bear is Persia (Iran).[4] This coincides with an image that Nebuchadnezzar sees in a dream that Daniel interprets. (Daniel 2).

Revelation 17: 9 – 12 explains the symbolism of the seven heads and ten horns.

Revelation 17: 9 – 12

9   And here is the mind which hath wisdom. The seven heads are seven mountains, on which the woman sitteth.

10 And there are seven kings: five are fallen, and one is, and the other is not yet come; and when he cometh, he must continue a short space.

11 And the beast that was, and is not, even he is
the eighth, and is of the seven, and goeth into
perdition.

12 And the ten horns which thou sawest are ten
kings, which have received no kingdom as yet;
but receive power as kings...

The heads are seven mountains and there are seven kings. Some
have said the seven mountains refer to Rome that has seven hills.
However, mountains are kingdoms that have kings. The image
Nebuchadnezzar sees in Daniel 2 has a head of gold which is Babylon.
(Daniel tells Nebuchadnezzar it is him, and he is over Babylon.) The
image has a breast and arms of silver. (The next kingdom was the
Medio-Persians.) The belly and thighs were brass, which is Greece.
The legs were legs of iron, and this is the Roman Empire. The feet are
iron mingled with clay. (Some say this is a revised Roman or Holy
Roman Empire.)

Another source says this is the Ottoman (Turkish) Empire,
which came after Rome, and will be revised with the restoring of
a caliphate.[4] In Daniel 2:35, it says that a stone hits the feet, and
the image crumbles. The stone becomes a great *mountain* that
filled the whole earth. In Daniel 2:44, it says that God will set up a
great *kingdom* that would break up all the other kingdoms. So the
mountain is a kingdom.

Daniel 2: 35, 44

35 Then was the iron, the clay, the brass, the
silver, and the gold, broken to pieces together,
and became like the chaff of the summer
threshingfloors; and the wind carried them
away, that no place was found for them: and
*the stone that smote the image became a great
mountain*, and filled the whole earth.

44 And in the days of these kings shall the *God of
heaven set up a kingdom*, which shall never be
destroyed: and the kingdom shall not be left
to othe people, *but it shall break in pieces and*

consume all these kingdoms, and it shall stand
for ever.

The mountains in Revelation 17:9 are not the Seven Hills of Rome; they are kingdoms. The kingdoms in Daniel are the same mentioned in Revelation 17. Five are fallen, and one is. The one in John's day is Rome. The five fallen (and these are kingdoms that impacted Israel) are: Egypt, Assyria, Babylon, Medio-Persia, and Greece. The sixth is Rome. Some say the seventh would be the British Empire and the eighth (which is of the seven) would be a revised Roman Empire. As stated earlier, the seventh could be the empire that came after Rome, which had an impact on Israel (The British Empire did not. Israel was no longer a nation after AD 70). This was the Ottoman (Turkish) Empire. The eighth could be either a revised Roman or as one source has said, Holy Roman Empire[3] or a revised caliphate. I wonder if there may not be a merging of Europe and Muslim nations. Many have taught that the Antichrist would come from the European Union, yet we see the potential rising of an Islamic caliphate. After all, many have said that it won't be too long before Europe is mostly Muslim. We may come to understand the significance of Arab nations as world events move us closer to the rule of the eighth beast. Things may be evident very soon as we see that world powers can be changed seemingly overnight.

We see in Revelation 17:12 that the ten horns are ten kings who are given power with the beast for a time.

Verse 3. (Rev. 13) One of the heads is wounded. In Revelation 17, the seven heads are mountains, and as shown, the mountains are kingdoms. Some think that the Antichrist will get wounded in the head, die, and be healed. Since mountains are kingdoms, it is referring to a kingdom being destroyed (such as the Roman Empire or the Muslim caliphate) and then revised. I had said previously that sometimes, John gets an explanation of what he is seeing. When this happens, the puzzle pieces fit together nicely.

Verse 5. This eighth beast, the king of the last kingdom (before Jesus's kingdom) blasphemes God, and he rules for three and a half years. You will see that Revelation does not mention seven years.

Yet if you have ever heard of the Great Tribulation, it has always been discussed as seven years. Seven years comes from a teaching from Daniel 9 of a week in Bible prophecy. The teaching is that there will be a treaty signed, which is derived from the term "confirm the covenant" between the Antichrist and Israel, and this will begin the week or seven years. If there were to be a treaty signed, it may be that the first three and a half years will be a seemingly great time of peace until the Antichrist breaks the covenant, and the three and a half years of a Great Tribulation begins. I am not going to go into detail about Daniel and his discussion of seventy weeks, sixty-nine weeks, and one week. I do not have revelation knowledge and would only be repeating others' teaching. What I am saying is I do not know (yet).

Verse 7. The Antichrist makes war with the saints and overcomes them. Further, in Revelation, we will see saints in heaven that overcame the beast. Power is given to him over all nations. Some nations may try to fight him, but he will exercise power. This isn't John saying this. He is repeating what he heard. Some say the Antichrist will only rule in the Middle East because this is "all" to John. However, God is aware of other nations.

Verse 8. All will worship him whose names are not in the Lamb's book of life. Those whose names are in the Lamb's book of life (born-again believers) will not worship the beast, and we will see later some will be beheaded. Again, God is saying all peoples of the earth will be required to take this mark.

Revelation 13: 10 – 18

10 He that leadeth into captivity shall go into captivity: he that killeth with the sword must be killed with the sword. Here is the patience and the faith of the saints.

11 And I beheld another beast coming up out of the earth; and he had two horns like a lamb, and he spake as a dragon.

12 And he exerciseth all the power of the first beast before him, and causeth the earth and

them which dwell therein to worship the first beast, whose deadly wound was healed.

13 And he doeth great wonders, so that he maketh fire come down from heaven on the earth in the sight of men,

14 And deceiveth them that dwell on the earth by the means of those miracles which he had power to do in the sight of the beast; saying to them that dwell on the earth, that they should make an image to the beast, which had the wound by a sword, and did live.

15 And he had power to give life unto the image of the beast, that the image of the beast should both speak, and cause that as many as would not worship the image of the beast should be killed.

16 And he causeth all, both small and great, rich and poor, free and bond, to receive a mark in their right hand, or in their foreheads:

17 And that no man might buy or sell, save he that had the mark, or the name of the beast, or the number of his name.

18 Here is wisdom. Let him that hath understanding count the number of the beast: for it is the number of a man; and his number is Six hundred threescore and six.

Verses 11–12. There is another beast that exercises the power of the first beast. (This could be the eighth, which is of the seven.) He causes people to worship the first beast.

Verses 13–14. He does great wonders and miracles. He can cause fire to come down from heaven, and he will deceive people because of the miracles. This is the person we refer to as the Antichrist. He has an image made to the first beast.

Verse 15. He has power to give life to the image of the beast and power to make it speak. This is a new beast that makes an image of the old beast. Could this image be a clone that is made to speak or artificial intelligent android? Those who do not worship the beast will be killed.

Verse 16. He causes all to receive a mark in their right hand or forehead.

Verses 17–18. No one can buy or sell without the mark, the name of the beast, or the number of his name (remember we saw earlier in Revelation 13 that the beast had a name of blasphemy and blasphemed the God of heaven.) Since no one can buy or sell, it suggests an economic system, very likely a one-world economic system. It may be a cashless society in which a chip is placed in the hand or forehead that can be scanned. All banking information, health information, and immigration status will be on this chip. This sounds good on the surface. If the information on the chip could be scrambled, it would prevent identity theft, and we wouldn't even have to carry around a credit card or insurance cards. This technology is already available and has been tested. In order to be a part of the beast system, you are going to have to commit to worship the beast. You may have to invoke the name of blasphemy. The number of the beast is 666. The number of a man is six. Some have used a system of numerology to come up with names and have come up with many different people. One source gives a fascinating explanation of the meaning of 666.[4] If what this source has recognized is revelation knowledge of the number 666, then the beast system has been revealed, and we may be much closer to end-time events than we ever imagined. It may very well be that the Antichrist is alive today and could be revealed anytime. The actual ruler is not known yet, but it would mean we know exactly what the 666 is. It would take someone who knows Arabic to discover this. We have seen that with radical (which is actually, fundamental) Islam, if you don't acknowledge that Allah is God, you can get your head sawed off. This is happening in this present time. If this is the time of the end, then Islam has to play a role because they are the ones fulfilling the prophecies. John wrote Revelation in Greek, and the translators translated from Greek. There are words that show the

Greek, such as chi, sigma, etc. There are also Greek symbols. When John saw these symbols, he would have written what he saw, and the translators would have translated it from the Greek as 666. The symbols, looking almost exactly as the Greek symbols, if read from right to left in Arabic translates as "In the name of Allah," with cross swords in the front. The cross swords is the chi or first 6. This is definitely a name of blasphemy.

If this is the number of the beast or the beast's creed, there can still be a mark required in the hand or forehead to be part of the economy. How close could we be? Islam just may very well be the religion that the one world government chooses to adopt for everyone. I wonder if an understanding of 666 isn't one of the things we were told would be revealed in the end time. This certainly can place Revelation into our generation.

Revelation 14: 1 – 10

1   And I looked, and, lo, a Lamb stood on the mount Sion, and with him an hundred forty and four thousand, having his Father's name written in their foreheads.

2   And I heard a voice from heaven, as the voice of many waters, and as the voice of a great thunder: and I heard the voice of harpers harping with their harps:

3   And they sung as it were a new song before the throne, and before the four beasts, and the elders: and no man could learn that song but the hundred and forty and thousand, which were redeemed from the earth.

4   These are they which were not defiled with women; for they are virgins. These are they which follow the Lamb whithersoever he goeth. These were redeemed from among men, being the firstfruits unto God and to the Lamb.

5   And in their mouth was found no guile: for they are without fault before the throne of God.

6   And I saw another angel fly in the midst of heaven, having the everlasting gospel to preach unto them that dwell on the earth, and to every nation, and kindred, and tongue, and people,

7   Saying with a loud voice, Fear God, and give glory to him; for the hour of his judgment is come: and worship him that made heaven, and earth, and the sea, and the fountains of waters.

8   And there followed another angel, saying, Babylon is fallen, is fallen, that great city, because she made all nations drink of the wine of the wrath of her fornication.

9   And the third angel followed them, saying with a loud voice, If any man worship the beast and his image, and receive his mark in his forehead, or in his hand,

10 The same shall drink of the wine of the wrath of God, which is poured out without mixture into the cup of his indignation; and he shall be tormented with fire and brimstone in the presence of the holy angels, and in the presence of the Lamb:

Verses 1–4. We see the 144,000 mentioned again, marked by God in their foreheads. They sing a song no one else can learn. They were redeemed from the earth and weren't defiled with women. I think this refers to spiritual defilement. They don't commit spiritual adultery but remain true to the Lamb because they don't worship any other god. They are the firstfruits unto God. Firstfruits means first harvest.

Verse 6. The gospel is preached. This may be where some get that the 144,000 get saved and preach the gospel to others during the Great Tribulation.

Verse 8. This verse mentions the fall of Babylon. There is much more of this later in Revelation.

Verses 9–10. Any man who worships the beast and his image and receive his mark, (we already read that only those whose names are not in the Lamb's Book of Life take the mark), will drink of the wine of the wrath of God. We will see later that those who are not in the Lamb's Book of Life will be cast into the lake of fire. We know that those who are in the Lamb's Book of Life (they are saved) will not take the mark of the beast. They may be martyred by getting their heads cut off or be kept, but they do not take the mark and are not appointed to the wrath of God.

Revelation 14: 11 – 20

11 And the smoke of their torment ascendeth up for ever and ever: and they have no rest day nor night, who worship the beast and his image, and whosoever receiveth the mark of his name.

12 Here is the patience of the saints: here are they that keep the commandments of God, and the faith of Jesus.

13 And I heard a voice from heaven saying unto me, Write, Blessed are the dead which die in the Lord from henceforth: Yea, saith the Spirit, that they may rest from their labours; and their works do follow them.

14 And I looked, and behold a white cloud, and upon the cloud one sat like unto the Son of man, having on his head a golden crown, and in his hand a sharp sickle.

15 And another angel came out of the temple, crying with a loud voice to him that sat on the

cloud, Thrust in thy sickle, and reap: for the time is come for thee to reap; for the harvest of the earth is ripe.

16 And he that sat on the cloud thrust in his sickle on the earth; and the earth was reaped.

17 And another angel came out of the temple which is in heaven, he also having a sharp sickle.

18 And another angel came out from the altar, which had power over fire; and cried with a loud cry to him that had the sharp sickle, saying, Thrust in thy sharp sickle, and gather the clusters of the vine of the earth; for her grapes are fully ripe.

19 And the angel thrust in his sickle into the earth, and gathered the vine of the earth, and cast it into the great winepress of the wrath of God.

20 And the winepress was trodden without the city, and blood came out of the winepress, even unto the horse bridles, the space of a thousand and six hundred furlong.

Verse 11. It is still talking about those who take the mark of the beast. Notice it says they have no rest day or night. This contradicts a teaching that says that people cast into the lake of fire are permanently consumed and will not suffer. Someone asked me one time if I had ever heard of something being burned in a fire and not being consumed. My answer was the burning bush that Moses saw. I got a blank stare when I gave the answer.

Exodus 3:2

2 And the angel of the Lord appeared unto him in a flame of fire out of the midst of a bush: and he looked, and, behold, the bush burned with fire, and the bush was not consumed.

Verses 12 – 13. "Here is the patience of the saints". We see that those who die in the Lord are blessed. As was stated earlier, pre-trib rapture teaching is that after Revelation 3, the church is no longer mentioned, so the church is not present. If the rapture is pre-trib, these could be believers that get saved during the Tribulation period. However, they are still a part of the body and church of Jesus Christ.

THE EARTH IS REAPED

There is something very interesting at this point.

Verses 14–16. John sees a white cloud with one like unto the Son of Man (Jesus) holding a sickle. The time is come to reap. *Now? Not before the Tribulation?* He reaps the harvest from the earth. What is this? What is a raising up of those who are alive and remain doing after the mark of the beast and as people are being drawn to the battle of Armageddon?

Verses 17–20. Another angel gathers people into the winepress of the wrath of God. Blood comes out of the winepress. The winepress of the wrath of God presses out blood, not wine. This we understand to be the battle of Armageddon.

See if you notice a parallel from this parable of Jesus to the vision that John sees of the sickles.

Matthew 13: 24 – 30, 36 – 43

24 Another parable put he forth unto them, saying, The kingdom of heaven is likened unto a man which sowed good seed in his field:

25 But while men slept, his enemy came and sowed tares among the wheat, and went his way.

26 But when the blade was sprung up, and brought forth fruit, then appeared the tares also.

27 So the servants of the householder came and said unto him, Sir, didst not thou sow good

seed in thy field? from whence then hath it tares?

28 He said unto them, An enemy hath done this. The servants said unto him, Wilt thou then that we go and gather them up?

29 But he said, Nay; lest while ye gather up the tares, ye root up also the wheat with them.

30 Let both grow together until the harvest: and in the time of harvest I will say to the reapers, Gather ye together first the tares, and bind them in bundles to burn them: but gather the wheat into my barn.

36 Then Jesus sent the multitude away, and went into the house: and his disciples came unto 1 him, saying, Declare unto us the parable of the tares of the field.

37 He answered and said unto them, He that soweth the good seed is the Son of man;

38 The field is the world; the good seed are the children of the kingdom; but the tares are the children of the wicked one;

39 The enemy that sowed them is the devil; the harvest is the end of the world; and the reapers are the angels.

40 As therefore the tares are gathered and burned in the fire; so shall it be in the end of this world.

41 The Son of man shall send forth his angels, and they shall gather out of his kingdom all things that offend, and them which do iniquity;

42 And shall cast them into a furnace of fire: there shall be wailing and gnashing of teeth.

43 Then shall the righteous shine forth as the
   sun in the kingdom of their Father. Who hath
   ears to hear, let him hear.

Verses 37–38. He who sows the good seed is the Son of Man. (The Son of man had the sickle). The field is the world.

Verse 39. The harvest is the end of the world, and the reapers are the angels.

Verse 40. As the tares are gathered and burned, so shall it be in the end of the world.

Verse 41. The Son of Man shall gather out of his kingdom all things that offend.

Verse 43. Then shall the righteous shine forth in the kingdom of their Father. (After Jesus comes he sets up His kingdom and we rule and reign with Him.) At the end of this book is discussion of the end of the thousand-year reign and the Great White Throne judgment. This parable could be referring to this time.

CHAPTER 8

Winding Up

Revelation 15

1 And I saw another sign in heaven, great and marvellous, seven angels having the seven last plagues; for in them is filled up the wrath of God.

2 And I saw as it were a sea of glass mingled with fire: and them that had gotten the victory over the beast, and over his image, and over his mark, and over the number of his name, stand on the sea of glass, having the harps of God.

3 And they sing the song of Moses the servant of God, and the song of the Lamb, saying, Great and marvellous are thy works, Lord God Almighty; just and true are thy ways, thou King of saints.

4 Who shall not fear thee, O Lord, and glorify thy name? for thou only art holy: for all nations shall come and worship before thee; for thy judgments are made manifest.

5 And after that I looked, and, behold, the temple of the tabernacle of the testimony in heaven was opened:

6 And the seven angels came out of the temple, having the seven Plagues, clothed in pure and

white linen, and having their breasts girded with golden girdles.

7   And one of the four beasts gave unto the seven angels seven golden vials full of the wrath of God, who liveth for ever and ever.

8   And the temple was filled with smoke from the glory of God, and from his power; and no man was able to enter into the temple, till the seven plagues of the seven angels were fulfilled.

THE SEVEN LAST PLAGUES

Verses 1-7. This scripture passage refers to the seven last plagues which are "filled with the wrath of God" or the vials of the wrath of God as they are called in Rev. 16:1. This is the third section of the pirate's telescope. It was discussed previously that believers are not subject to the wrath of God. It is for this reason that many believe the church must be raptured before these are poured out. However, God shows us with the 144,000 that people can be kept from hurt on the earth without having to be raptured. We will see that it isn't until the seventh vial of the wrath of God that Jesus comes.

Some of these seven last plagues are addressed specifically to those who take the mark of the beast. Others seem to be a finishing up, so to speak, or a culmination of the seven trumpets. The seven trumpets show a third of the sea creatures die, and with the vial of wrath, all creatures die.

Verse 8. John sees a sea of glass and those who had gained victory over the beast. "Sea" refers to people. Perhaps these got victory because they had strength to refuse the mark even though they were martyred for the refusal.

The temple is filled with smoke so that no man could enter until the seven plagues were fulfilled. Perhaps, these seven plagues happen very quickly.

Revelation 16: 1 – 11

1 And I heard a great voice out of the temple saying to the seven angels, Go your ways, and pour out the vials of the wrath of God upon the earth.

2 And the first went, and poured out his vial upon the earth; and there fell a noisome and grievous sore upon the men which had the mark of the beast, and upon them which worshipped his image.

3 And the second angel poured out his vial upon the sea; and it became as the blood of a dead man: and every living soul died in the sea.

4 And the third angel poured out his vial upon the rivers and fountains of waters; and they became blood.

5 And I heard the angel of the waters say, Thou art righteous, O Lord, which art, and wast, and shalt be, because thou hast judged thus.

6 For they have shed the blood of saints and prophets, and thou hast given them blood to drink; for they are worthy.

7 And I heard another out of the altar say, Even so, Lord God Almighty, true and righteous are thy judgments.

8 And the fourth angel poured out his vial upon the sun; and power was given unto him to scorch men with fire.

9 And men were scorched with great heat, and blasphemed the name of God, which hath power over these plagues: and they repented not to give him glory.

10 And the fifth angel poured out his vial upon the seat of the beast; and his kingdom was full

of darkness; and they gnawed their tongues for pain,

11 And blasphemed the God of heaven because of their pains and their sores, and repented not of their deeds.

Verse 2. The first vial is a sore on those who have the mark of the beast. Could whatever the mark is, such as an implant, cause an immune reaction that causes sores?

Verse 3. The sea becomes blood and every soul dies. With the trumpets, it was one-third of the sea that becomes blood and one-third of the creatures in the sea die. Things may have just continued to get worse since the trumpets sounded. I have addressed the fact that there is an algae that creates a red "toxic bloom" that kills all organisms which are exposed to it. Recently it was said in a documentary that people saw 100,000 sea creatures washed up dead across the world in one year, including in the United States. The eating of shell fish was banned in certain areas in California because of this. It was said that this toxic bloom is continuing to affect greater areas. This will add to threats of famine especially on peoples that greatly depend on fishing for a food source.

Verse 4. The rivers become blood also. It is frightening to think of living in a time when there is no life in the oceans and rivers. In the time of Moses, when the Nile became as blood, people had to dig down further in the earth to find water. Water is going to become an extremely scarce commodity.

Verses 8-9. The fourth vial is poured out on the sun. Earlier scriptures speak of the sun being darkened and here the sun scorches with a great heat. Perhaps there will be super solar flares, or the ozone layer is destroyed. Despite all the problems, people still do not repent and blaspheme God instead.

Verse 10. After scorching heat, the fifth angel brings darkness on the beast and his kingdom.

Revelation 16: 12 – 21

12 And the sixth angel poured out his vial upon the great river Euphrates; and the water thereof was dried up, that the way of the kings of the east might be prepared.

13 And I saw three unclean spirits like frogs come out of the mouth of the dragon, and out of the mouth of the beast, and out of the mouth of the false prophet.

14 For they are the spirits of devils, working miracles, which go forth unto the kings of the earth and of the whole world, to gather them to the battle of that great day of God Almighty.

15 Behold, I come as a thief. Blessed is he that watcheth, and keepeth his garments, lest he walk naked, and they see his shame.

16 And he gathered them together into a place called in the Hebrew tongue Armageddon.

17 And the seventh angel poured out his vial into the air; and there came a great voice out of the temple of heaven, from the throne, saying, It is done.

18 And there were voices, and thunders, and lightnings; and there was a great earthquake, such as was not since men were upon the earth, so mighty an earthquake, and so great.

19 And the great city was divided into three parts, and the cities of the nations fell: and great Babylon came in remembrance before God, to give unto her the cup of the wine of the fierceness of his wrath.

20 And every island fled away, and the mountains were not found.

21 And there fell upon men a great hail out of heaven, every stone about the weight of a talent: and men blasphemed God because of the plague of the hail; for the plague thereof was exceeding great.

Verse 12. The sixth vial is poured out and we see the similarities with the sixth trumpet. We close the telescope back up. We see that the Euphrates River is dried up so that "kings of the east" can cross. Remember I spoke of a dam on the Euphrates River and that China is a king of the east.

Verses 13 – 14. Three unclean spirits as frogs come out of the mouth of the dragon (Satan, as we saw in Rev. 12), the beast (the antichrist), and his false prophet. (This may be the religious leader of the antichrist kingdom). These go into the world to gather people to the battle of Armageddon. Remember the angel with the sickle does the same thing in Rev. 14.

Verses 15 – 16. "Behold I come as a thief." If you have a red-letter edition of the Bible, meaning the words of Jesus are in red, you will see that this verse is in red. It is Jesus speaking. What is He doing coming as a thief now? I thought He came as a thief before the Tribulation to rapture the church and take them to heaven. Coming as a thief does not mean that He sneaks down, and no one sees Him. As I previously stated, it means that no one knows the day or hour. Jesus said that if a man knew the thief was coming he would watch for him. (Matt. 24:43). He "gathers them together" to Armageddon. This is where the "battle of Armageddon" (or Megiddo) takes place.

Verses 17 – 21. With the seventh vial it is said, "It is done." With the seventh trumpet and the seventh vial Jesus comes. There are thunders lightenings, and a great earthquake "such as was not since men were upon the earth." The great earthquake is not one of many it is unique. The city (Jerusalem) is divided. Remember that in Zechariah 14 it says that Mt. Olives will split at Jesus' coming. Cities of the nation's fall. Babylon is mentioned. The next few chapters discuss Babylon and its fall. Some comment that Babylon is the city that is divided and others refer to Jerusalem as spiritual Babylon.

Still others say it is Rome. As I read it, it seems that the city that is divided is Jerusalem and Babylon is a different matter. I will go into more discussion of Babylon in the next sections. Notice the islands "fled" away, and the mountains are not found. (We saw this in Rev. 6 with the sixth seal.) This shows us again how we can process what is happening in the book of Revelation by the sequence of events. There is great hail. I read that the weight of a talent is over 100 pounds. Imagine 100 pound hail falling to the earth.

Revelation 17: 1 – 9

1   And there came one of the seven angels which had the seven vials, and talked with me, saying unto me, come hither; I will shew unto thee the judgment of the great whore that sitteth upon many waters:

2   With whom the kings of the earth have committed fornication, and inhabitants of the earth have been made drunk with the wine of her fornication.

3   So he carried me away in the spirit into the wilderness: and I saw a woman sit upon a scarlet coloured beast, full of names of blasphemy, having seven heads and ten horns.

4   And the woman was arrayed in purple and scarlet colour, and decked with gold and precious stones and pearls, having a golden cup in her hand full of abominations and filthiness of her fornication:

5   And upon her forehead was a name written, MYSTERY, BABYLON THE GREAT, THE MOTHER OF HARLOTS AND ABOMINATIONS OF THE EARTH.

6   And I saw the woman drunken with the blood of the saints, and with the blood of the martyrs

of Jesus: and when I saw her, I wondered with great admiration.

7 And the angel said unto me, wherefore didst thou marvel? I will tell thee the mystery of the woman, and of the beast that carrieth her, which hath the seven heads and ten horns.

8 The beast that thou sawest was, and is not; and shall ascend out of the bottomless pit, and go into perdition: and they that dwell on the earth shall wonder, whose names were not written in the book of life from the foundation of the world, when they behold the beast that was, and is not, and yet is.

9 And here is the mind which hath wisdom. The seven heads are seven mountains, on which the woman sitteth.

MYSTERY BABYLON

Verse 5. Babylon was an actual city. Very early, the tower of Babel showed a world system that wanted to reach to heaven, and God scattered people to slow their arrogant imagination. This story can be found in Genesis 11. The children of Israel eventually go into captivity to Babylon. Daniel was in captivity in Babylon. The figure that Nebuchadnezzar saw in a dream had a head of gold which represented the Babylonian (Chaldean) kingdom. The city of Babylon was in what is now modern day Iraq. Verse 5 refers to the Mystery Babylon, the Mother of Harlots. Verse 2 states, "With whom the kings of the earth have committed fornication." This means spiritual adultery in which they worship the false god instead of God. In verse 3, we see her sitting on a beast (the same beast as mentioned earlier, full of blasphemy and having seven heads and ten horns). This Mystery Babylon is part of the beast kingdom. Verse 9 mentions the seven mountains. Some say this is the Catholic Church because this is referring to the Seven Hills of Rome. Remember we discussed that the seven mountains are seven kingdoms, not the hills of Rome. Others have said the in the European Union (EU) there is actually a figure of a woman on a scarlet-colored beast (a cow) that is a symbol of the EU. There have actually been pictures of it in magazines. Some say that this is the whole world system beginning with the first kingdom. Just as there was a Babylonian kingdom and a city called Babylon during Daniel's time, there is a beast kingdom (perhaps a one-world political, economic, and religious system) and an actual city.

Revelation 17: 10 – 18

10 And there are seven kings: five are fallen, and one is, and the other is not yet come; and when he cometh, he must continue a short space.

11 And the beast that was, and is not, even he is the eighth, and is of the seven, and goeth into perdition.

12 And the ten horns which thou sawest are ten kings, which have received no kingdom as yet; but receive power as kings one hour with the beast.

13 These have one mind, and shall give their power and strength unto the beast.

14 These shall make war with the Lamb, and the Lamb shall overcome them: for he is Lord of lords, and King of kings: and they that are with him are called, and chosen, and faithful.

15 And he saith unto me, The waters which thou sawest, where the whore sitteth, are peoples, and multitudes, and nations, and tongues.

16 And the ten horns which thou sawest upon the beast, these shall hate the whore, and shall make her desolate and naked, and shall eat her flesh, and burn her with fire.

17 For God hath put in their hearts to fulfil his will, and to agree, and give their kingdom

unto the beast, until the words of God shall be fulfilled.

18 And the woman which thou sawest is that great city, which reigneth over the kings of the earth.

THE JUDGMENT OF MYSTERY BABYLON

Verses 10–18. These verses give a further explanation of the woman and the beast on which she sits. From the description we see that the beast is a seven-headed, ten-horned antichrist kingdom mentioned in Rev 12. The waters on which the Mystery Babylon sits are peoples, multitudes, nations. This shows the extent of the antichrist's kingdom. There were ten horns or ten kings that were given power with the beast (Rev 17:12). In verse 18 we are told that the woman is "that great city" which reigns over the kings of the earth. I heard one person say that this is New York City. Later, we will see that she has in her the blood of martyrs and saints. I do not know of New York City ever killing saints and creating martyrs. If she became the capital of the one-world government this could become the case. In John's day, we would think the great city would be Rome. Perhaps there will be a newly built city that is even called Babylon.

In verse 14 we see that the ten kings will make war with the Lamb (Jesus) but Jesus will overcome them.

Revelation 18: 1 – 12

1 And after these things I saw another angel come down from heaven, having great power; and the earth was lightened with his glory.

2 And he cried mightily with a strong voice, saying, Babylon the great is fallen, is fallen, and is become the habitation of devils, and the hold of every foul spirit, and a cage of every unclean and hateful bird.

3 For all nations have drunk of the wine of the wrath of her fornication, and the kings of the earth have committed fornication with her, and the merchants of the earth are waxed rich through the abundance of her delicacies.

4 And I heard another voice from heaven, saying, Come out of her, my people, that ye be not partakers of her sins, and that ye receive not of her plagues.

5 For her sins have reached unto heaven, and God hath remembered her iniquities.

6 Reward her even as she rewarded you, and double unto her double according to her works: in the cup which she hath filled fill to her double.

7 How much she hath glorified herself, and lived deliciously, so much torment and sorrow give her: for she saith in her heart, I sit a queen, and am no widow, and shall see no sorrow.

8 Therefore shall her plagues come in one day, death, and mourning, and famine; and she shall be utterly burned with fire: for strong is the Lord God who judgeth her.

9 And the kings of the earth, who have committed fornication and lived deliciously with her, shall bewail her, and lament for her, when they shall see the smoke of her burning,

10 Standing afar off for the fear of her torment, saying, Alas, alas, that great city Babylon, that mighty city! For in one hour is thy judgment come.

11 And the merchants of the earth shall weep and mourn over her; for no man buyeth their merchandise any more:

12 The merchandise of gold, and silver, and precious stones, and of pearls, and fine linen, and purple, and silk, and scarlet, and all thyine wood, and all manner vessels of ivory, and all manner vessels of most precious wood, and of brass, and iron, and marble.

This just shows that Babylon will fall: The city and/or the world system. It may also include the world religion. If this is the system of the mark of the beast (the woman sits on the beast with seven heads and ten horns), then we do not want to be a part of this.

Verse 4 tells us to come out of her that you don't partake of her sins and receive her plagues. True believers must not partake of a one-world religion. If you are in a church that starts to teach doctrines of devils, or become a part of a one-world religion, get out.

Verse 10. In one hour, her judgment is come. This could just mean a short time.

Verse 12. Merchants shall weep over her. It discusses all the imports she took in.

Revelation 18: 13 – 24

13 And cinnamon, and odours, and ointments, and frankincense, and wine, and oil, and fine flour, and wheat, and beasts, and sheep, and horses, and chariots, and slaves, and souls of men.

14 And the fruits that thy soul lusted after are departed from thee, and all things which were dainty and goodly are departed from thee, and thou shalt find them no more at all.

15 The merchants of these things, which were made rich by her, shall stand afar off for the fear of her torment, weeping and wailing,

16 And saying, alas, alas, that great city, that was clothed in fine linen, and purple, and scarlet,

and decked with gold, and precious stones, and pearls!

17 For in one hour so great riches is come to nought. And every shipmaster, and all the company in ships, and sailors, and as many as trade by sea, stood afar off,

18 And cried when they saw the smoke of her burning, saying, what city is like unto this great city!

19 And they cast dust on their heads, and cried, weeping and wailing, saying, Alas, alas, that great city, wherein were made rich all that had ships in the sea by reason of her costliness! For in one hour is she made desolate?

20 Rejoice over her, thou heaven, and ye holy apostles and prophets; for God hath avenged you on her.

21 And a mighty angel took up a stone like a great millstone, and cast it into the sea, saying, Thus with violence shall that great city Babylon be thrown down, and shall be found no more at all.

22 And the voice of harpers, and musicians, and of pipers, and trumpeters, shall be heard no more at all in thee; and no craftsman, of whatsoever craft he be, shall be found any more in thee; and the sound of a millstone shall be heard no more at all in thee;

23 And the light of a candle shall shine no more at all in thee; and the voice of the bridegroom and of the bride shall be heard no more at all in thee: for thy merchants were the great men of the earth; for by thy sorceries were all nations deceived.

24 And in her was found the blood of prophets,
and of saints, and of all that were slain upon
the earth.

The rest of chapter 18 continues, showing the destruction of the
Mystery Babylon and how the trade is gone and people morn over
her. All of this may be representative of the point that when Jesus
comes, He takes authority over all nations and people, ends the old
world system, and sets up his rule and reign. All cities and nations
will change how they function, and they will be based on God's laws
and kingdom rules and principles. As we will see in Revelation 19,
Jesus is the one who judged the woman.

Revelation 19: 1 – 10

1 And after these things I heard a great voice
of much people in heaven, saying, Alleluia;
Salvation, and glory, and honour, and power,
unto the Lord our God:

2 For true and righteous are his judgments: for
he hath judged the great whore, which did
corrupt the earth with her fornication, and
hath avenged the blood of his servants at her
hand.

3 And again they said, Alleluia. And her smoke
rose up for ever and ever.

4 And the four and twenty elders and the four
beasts fell down and worshipped God that sat
on the throne, saying, Amen; Alleluia.

5 And a voice came out of the throne, saying,
Praise our God, all ye his servants, and ye that
fear him, both small and great.

6 And I heard as it were the voice of a great
multitude, and as the voice of many waters,
and as the voice of mighty thunderings,
saying, alleluia: for the Lord God omnipotent
reigneth.

7   Let us be glad and rejoice, and give honour to him: for the marriage of the Lamb is come, and his wife hath made herself ready.

8   And to her was granted that she should be arrayed in fine linen, clean and white: for the fine linen is the righteousness of saints.

9   And he saith unto me, Write, Blessed are they which are called unto the marriage supper of the Lamb. And he saith unto me, these are the true sayings of God.

10   And I fell at his feet to worship him. And he said unto me, See thou do it not: I am thy fellowservant, and of thy brethren that have the testimony of Jesus: worship God: for the testimony of Jesus is the spirit of prophecy.

The first part of chapter 19 is worship to God for the judgment of the Mystery Babylon, and that she has been destroyed.

Verses 7–9. The marriage of the Lamb is come. The bride has made herself ready. Some teach a long preparation in heaven of seven years for the bride to get ready. In verse 8, she is given fine linen, clean and white, for the fine linen is the righteousness of the saints. Born-again believers are told that we are made the righteousness of God in Christ Jesus (2 Cor. 5:21). We are only righteous because He is righteous. If you study the preparation a Jewish bride undergoes to prepare for her husband (the herbs and cleansings), these are all types and shadows of the work Jesus does in us. Could it be that the bride made herself ready through receiving salvation through the shed blood of Jesus? As we put on resurrected bodies in the rapture, we are now able to be the completed bride. I have heard it said that Jesus is coming back for a glorious church without spot or wrinkle. But a close look at the scripture shows that He will *present us* as a glorious church. We will certainly be glorious when we all have resurrected bodies the same as Jesus.

Ephesians 5:27

27 That he might *present it* to himself a glorious church, not having spot, or wrinkle, or any such thing, but that it should be holy and without blemish.

We may never see a glorious unified church on the earth before Jesus' coming. Right at the time of the marriage supper of the Lamb, John sees Jesus coming. If the rapture occurs here, so does the changing to an immortal body. The marriage has come. It says in verse 9, "Blessed are they which are called unto the marriage supper of the Lamb." Could it be that the rapture itself is the calling to the marriage supper of the Lamb? Jesus prayed that the church would all be one (John 17:21). Perhaps this will be fulfilled in the new heaven and new earth in the New Jerusalem.

2 Peter 3:13

13 Nevertheless we, according to his promise, look for new heavens and a new earth, wherein dwelleth righteousness.

Revelation 19:11 – 21

11 And I saw heaven opened, and behold a white horse; and he that sat upon him was called Faithful and True, and in righteousness he doth judge and make war.

12 His eyes were as a flame of fire, and on his head were many crowns; and he had a name written, that no man knew, but he himself.

13 And he was clothed with a vesture dipped in blood: and his name is called The Word of God.

14 And the armies which were in heaven followed him upon white horses, clothed in fine linen, white and clean.

15 And out of his mouth goeth a sharp sword, that with it he should smite the nations: and

he shall rule them with a rod of iron: and he treadeth the winepress of the fierceness and wrath of Almighty God.

16 And he hath on his vesture and on his thigh a name written, KING OF KINGS, AND Lord OF LORDS.

17 And I saw an angel standing in the sun; and he cried with a loud voice, saying to all the fowls that fly in the midst of heaven, Come and gather yourselves together unto the supper of the great God;

18 That ye may eat the flesh of kings, and the flesh of captains, and the flesh of mighty men, and the flesh of horses, and of them that sit on them, and the flesh of all men, both free and bond, both small and great.

19 And I saw the beast, and the kings of the earth, and their armies, gathered together to make war against him that sat on the horse, and against his army.

20 And the beast was taken, and with him the false prophet that wrought miracles before him, with which he deceived them that had received the mark of the beast, and them that worshipped his image. These both were cast alive into a lake of fire burning with brimstone.

21 And the remnant were slain with the sword of him that sat upon the horse, which sword proceeded out of his mouth: and all the fowls were filled with their flesh.

COMING OF THE LORD

Verse 11. John has a vision of Jesus on a white horse. (In verse 16 he is King of kings, and in verse 15 he has a sword in his mouth).

Verses 12 – 13. These descriptions let us know that this is Jesus. Jesus had a name written that only he knows. Remember we learned in Rev. 3:12 that Jesus had a new name. His name is called the Word of God. (We know that Jesus is the Word made flesh, John 1:14.)

Verses 17–18. There is a marriage supper of the Lamb, and there is a supper of the great God. The supper of God is the fowls of the air called to eat of the flesh of those destroyed in the battle of Armageddon. The almost identical group of people whom the fowls eat is mentioned in Revelation 6 at the sixth seal.

Verse 19. The beast and the kings of the earth and their armies gather to make war against Jesus and His armies. It was pointed out earlier that spirits as frogs and the angel with the sickle have drawn kings and armies to this battle.

Revelation 16: 16, 19

16 And he gathered them together into a place called in the Hebrew tongue Armageddon.

19 And the great city was divided into three parts, and the cities of the nations fell: and great Babylon came in remembrance before God, to give unto her the cup of the wine of the fierceness of his wrath.

Verses 20–21. The beast (Antichrist) and false prophet are cast into the lake of fire. The others are destroyed with the sword (Word) in Jesus's mouth and their carcasses are eaten by vultures.

This is a vision that John is seeing of Jesus on a white horse. Does this mean that Jesus is coming back on a white horse? I have heard ministers say that Jesus is coming back on a horse. We have to remember that this is a vision. John had a vision of the four horses in Revelation 6. Do we expect to see a red horse riding around when war occurs, or a grim reaper on a pale horse every time someone dies? No. We understand these are symbolic and represent events. I heard a teaching that the difference between a dream and a vision is that a dream has to be interpreted and a vision is seeing something as it actually is and does not need an interpretation. This is not always the case. Joseph, Mary's husband, had a dream and was told specifically to take Mary and Jesus and flea to Egypt because Herod wanted to kill him (Matt. 2:13). Although dreams are often filled with symbolism, in this instance, there was no need for interpretation. Acts 10:1–28 relates that Peter had a vision of a sheet filled with unclean animals and was told to kill and eat them. Being Jewish, he said he couldn't do this because he never ate anything unclean. He was told not to call unclean what God has made clean. He saw the sheet three times. Cornelius' (a Gentile) servant came and told Peter that God said to get him to speak to Cornelius' house. Peter then understood the meaning of the vision. God wanted the gospel given to a Gentile and Peter was not to consider him unclean. I am certain that Peter did not go to lunch and ask the cook to make him a "pig in a blanket" because he had a vision of unclean animals on a sheet and was told to eat them. Visions sometimes have to be interpreted. The difference between a dream and a vision is simply that a dream occurs when a person is asleep. With a vision, the person is awake. The point is that John had a vision that needs to be understood as a vision and not necessarily taken literally. Jesus doesn't have a literal sword in His mouth. The sword represents Word that He speaks out of His mouth. In Zechariah 14:4, Jesus's feet will stand on Mt. Olives when he returns. If He returns on a horse, either Jesus has long legs, or it is a little horse (unless He hops off the horse).

There is another scripture that tells us specifically how Jesus is returning.

Acts 1: 9 – 11

9 And when he had spoken these things, while they beheld, he was taken up; and a cloud received him out of their sight.

10 And while they looked stedfastly toward heaven as he went up, behold, two men stood by them in white apparel;

11 Which also said, Ye men of Galilee, why stand ye gazing up into heaven? this same Jesus, which is taken up from you into heaven, shall

so come in like manner as ye have seen him go
into heaven.

We are told that Jesus was taken up in a cloud. The angel said that the same Jesus would come in like manner. He did not go up on a horse, so he is not returning on a horse. God could have shown Him going up on a horse if He had wanted us to understand that was how He was returning. Elisha saw a chariot and horses when Elijah went up to heaven (2 Kings 2:11). If the Antichrist tries to add to deception by riding into Jerusalem on a horse, we can know this is not scriptural.

CHAPTER 9

Jesus' Prophecies of End-time Events

Matthew 24, Mark 13, Luke 17, Luke 21 have reference to Jesus' prophetic Words of end-time events. I will just be addressing certain sections in these scriptures.

Matthew 24: 2 – 3, 6 – 8, 12 – 14, 21 – 22

2   And Jesus said unto them, See ye not all these things? Verily I say unto you, There shall not be left here one stone upon another, that shall not be thrown down.

3   And as he sat upon the mount of Olives, the disciples came unto him privately, saying, Tell us, when shall these things be? and what shall be the sign of thy coming, and of the end of the world?

6   And ye shall hear of wars and rumours of wars: see that ye be not troubled: for all these things must come to pass, but the end is not yet.

7   For nation shall rise against nation, and kingdom against kingdom: and there shall be famines, and pestilences, and earthquakes, in divers places.

8   All these are the beginning of sorrows.

12 And because iniquity shall abound, the love of many shall wax cold.

13 But he that shall endure unto the end, the same shall be saved.

14 And this gospel of the kingdom shall be preached in all the world for a witness unto all nations; and then shall the end come.

21 For then shall be great tribulation, such as was not since the beginning of the world to this time, no, nor ever shall be.

22 And except those days should be shortened, there should no flesh be saved: but for the elect's sake those days shall be shortened.

Verse 2. Jesus says the temple would be destroyed. This was fulfilled in AD 70.

Verse 3. Jesus is speaking from Mt. Olives. This is the same place that Zechariah says Jesus will set His feet when He returns. Jesus' disciples ask when the temple will be destroyed and what would be the sign of His coming and the end of the world. (Other translations use the word age for world.)

Verses 6–7. Jesus says there will be wars and rumors of war, nation against nation, and kingdom against kingdom. Some translations say, "Ethnic groups against ethnic groups." There will be famines, pestilences (plagues, disease), and earthquakes." Someone may say there have always been earthquakes. A specific source[3] researched the occurrence of earthquakes since the 1900s. From the 1900s until 2000, of earthquakes 6 or greater on the Richter scale, which is a large earthquake, there was an average of 43 per decade. From the year 2000 until 2010, there were 435. To go from 43 every ten years for one hundred years and then jump ten times to 435 shows there is great disturbance along the tectonic plates on the earth's crust.

Verse 8. These are the beginning of sorrows (or birth pangs).

Verse 12. Because iniquity shall abound the love of many shall wax cold. Remember there will be an apostasy.

Verse 13. Those who endure unto the end shall be saved. In Luke 21:19, it says, "In your patience possess...your souls." Hang in there.

Verse 14. The gospel shall be preached in all the world. With satellite, the gospel is all over the world. Everyone may not have access to satellite. There still are people who have never heard the gospel. Nevertheless, the gospel does reach the whole world. When I would hear teaching on the "Signs of the Times", which is what these prophetic events are sometimes called, this would be a stopping point. It would be said that everything Jesus prophesied has come to pass. There is nothing left, so He can come back any minute. The problem with this point of view is that Jesus doesn't stop here with the signs. He mentions more things that will happen before His coming. We can take notice that He does not mention here in these scriptures as one of the signs that He will come in the air and get the saints at an earlier coming. Teachers who hold to a pre-trib rapture stop right here because (although there is no break in Jesus' discussion of events) happenings in the Tribulation period are mentioned. Verse 21 refers to the Great Tribulation. It is one of the signs He gave and it has not happened yet. There are still more of Jesus' signs to be fulfilled. He places this event in the same section as wars and pestilence and earthquakes and all the other "Signs of the Times." Pre-trib teachers have to stop here because to go on does not align with a pre-trib rapture.

Verse 22. Except those days be shortened for the elect's sake, no flesh will be saved. I always looked at this to mean that believer's would not be able to endure everything that happens (Verse 13) unless God ends things sooner than planned. I heard another perspective recently. It has only been in modern history that man has gained the capability of destroying all of mankind. God may have to end these days before we blow ourselves off the face of the earth in a nuclear holocaust.

Luke 21: 11, 25 – 28

> 11 And great earthquakes shall be in divers places, and famines, and pestilences; and fearful sights and great signs shall there be from heaven.

25 And there shall be signs in the sun, and in the moon, and in the stars; and upon the earth distress of nations, with perplexity; the sea and the waves roaring;

26 Men's hearts failing them for fear, and for looking after those things which are coming on the earth: for the powers of heaven shall be shaken.

27 And then shall they see the Son of man coming in a cloud with power and great glory.

28 And when these things begin to come to pass, then look up, and lift up your heads; for your redemption draweth nigh.

Verses 11, 25 – 26. Great earthquakes have been mentioned before. These scriptures show the magnitude of troubles that will be occurring.

Verse 27. They shall see the Son of Man coming in a cloud. In Revelation 1, remember we saw that when Jesus comes, every eye shall see Him.

Verse 28. When these things begin to come to pass, then look up. What things? All of these things, including verse 27. When we see Him begin to come in the cloud (when we begin to see the sign of the lightning shining from the east to the west), we are to look up because our redemption is near. We are getting ready to go up and receive a resurrected body. We won't have to hide from His face and ask for the rocks and mountains to fall on us as those who are not in Christ will do.

Matthew 24: 37 – 41, 28

37 But as the days of Noe were, so shall also the coming of the Son of man be.

38 For as in the days that were before the flood they were eating and drinking, marrying and giving in marriage, until the day that Noe entered into the ark,

39 And knew not until the flood came, and *took them all away*, so shall also the coming of the Son of man be.

40 Then shall two be in the field; the one shall be taken, and the other left.

41 Two women shall be grinding at the mill; the one shall be taken, and the other left.

28 For wheresoever the carcase is, there will the eagles be gathered together.

Luke 17: 26 – 29, 34 – 37

26 And as it was in the days of Noe, so shall it be also in the days of the Son of man.

27 They did eat, they drank, they married wives, they were given in marriage, until the day that Noe entered into the ark, and the flood came, and *destroyed them all.*

28 Likewise also as it was in the days of Lot; they did eat, they drank, they bought, they sold, they planted, they builded;

29 But the same day that Lot went out of Sodom it rained fire and brimstone from heaven, and destroyed them all.

34 I tell you, in that night there shall be two men in one bed; the one shall be taken, and the other shall be left.

35 Two women shall be grinding together; the one shall be taken, and the other left.

36 Two men shall be in the field; the one shall be taken, and the other left.

37 And they answered and said unto him, Where, Lord? And he said unto them, Wheresoever the body is, thither will the eagles be gathered together.

Verse 39 (Matt. 24). As it was in the days of Noah, the flood came and took them all away. In Luke 17:27 it is worded that the flood came and destroyed them all. The taken away were not Noah and his family. The taken away were the destroyed.

Verses 40 – 41. Many teach that this is the rapture, but this is not the case. Comparing the days of Noah to the end-time, Jesus says that two would be in the field, one shall be taken and the other left. Remember, we just saw that the taken in the days of Noah were the destroyed. The taken away in this passage are not the righteous going up in the rapture. In Luke 17: 34 – 27 where Jesus mentions two in the field, two in one bed, in verse 37, Jesus is asked, "Where, Lord?" (Where are they taken?) Jesus answered that where the body is, the eagles will be gathered together. The word body in Luke is from a Greek word soma, and it means body. If you compare this to Matthew 24:28, it says where the "carcase" is there will the eagles be gathered together. This word is translated from the Greek as carcass or dead flesh. In the side of one of my Bibles, it says vultures in place of eagles. What do vultures or eagles do with a carcass? What do they do with dead flesh? They eat them. If you look in Revelation, where in end-time can you think of a scripture where birds, vultures (fowls) are called to eat dead bodies, dead flesh? You may remember the "supper of the great God" at the battle of Armageddon, at the winepress of the wrath of God, when Jesus returns and destroys the armies with the "sword of His mouth." Fowls of the air are called to eat flesh.

The taken away are taken to the winepress of the wrath of God. Remember, the spirits as frogs, and the angel with the sickle are drawing people of the earth to the winepress of the wrath of God. Again, this is not referring to the righteous being raptured. Concerning the one taken and the other left, perhaps there will be a draft, or a lottery, or people will just be impressed to help the beast that they worship. However it happens, not everyone goes to battle. The others left will be those who do not go to the battle of Armageddon. People fight in wars; others stay home. Of those who do not die, they will be here after Jesus comes, and we will rule them with Jesus.

PRE-TRIB/POST-TRIB RAPTURE TABLE

Rapture: Coming of the Lord and gathering together of the body of Christ, including dead and living in new resurrected bodies.

Pre-Tribulation (Scriptures supporting a Pre-Trib rapture.)	Pending (Scriptures that need more verifying before placement.)	Post-tribulation (Scriptures supporting a Post-Trib rapture.)
		I Thess 4:13 – 18
		John 6:40, 44, 54
		2 Thess 2
I Thess 5:10 Wrath		I Thess 5:10 Wrath
Luke 21:36 Escape		Luke 21:36 Escape
Mark 13: 35		Mark 13: 35
		Matt 24: 29, 31
		I Cor 15:23
		I Cor 15:52
		Rev 14: 14 – 20

I am not going to add all of the scriptures that have been discussed. If you want to have a project and continue with finishing the table, I leave it to you. At this point, it would be dependent on what your perspective is concerning the rapture. You have probably discovered that you have not found in the scriptures a coming of the Lord other than His Second Coming at the battle of Armageddon. The scriptures do not establish a pre-trib rapture. For these two reasons, 1 Thessalonians 4:13–18 are off the pending column and only in the post-trib column. The same is with 2 Thessalonians 2 under the post-trib column along with the wrath scriptures.

Mark 13: 35 is part of the theme scripture which shows that whether He comes in the evening, midnight or morning, (pre, mid, or post-trib,) we need to be ready. I Corinthians 15:23 talks of Jesus being the firstfruits of the resurrection and the rest of us will be resurrected at His coming. I Corinthians 15:52 states that the resurrection will occur at the last trump. Revelation 14: 14 – 20 addresses the harvest of the earth: Jesus in a cloud gathering the righteous and another angel gathering others to the wine press of the wrath of God (the battle of Armageddon.)

If you were to just give someone the scriptures to read concerning the rapture, and the person never heard any teaching it seems they would just automatically place it at the time of Jesus' Second Coming which ends the battle of Armageddon and the Great Tribulation. Just the rapture event itself fits post-trib because it is where there is a coming. The scripture in Matthew 24 that says that immediately after the tribulation of those days, the elect would be gathered, fits under the post-trib column. It actually says the gathering together is post-trib. The whole scripture passage in Revelation of the sickle and gathering of the harvest supports a post-trib rapture.

I end this with Mark 13: 33 and 35 and the reminder to watch and pray. It is good to be aware of the possibilities so we are not caught unprepared.

Mark 13:33, 35

33 Take ye heed, *watch and pray:* for ye know not when the time is.

35 *Watch ye therefore: for ye know not when the master of the house cometh, at even, or at midnight, or at the cockcrowing, or in the morning:*

It would be unwise to just assume Jesus will come before we have to face hard times.

CHAPTER 10

The Glorious End: A New Beginning

Revelation 20: 1 – 10

1   And I saw an angel come down from heaven, having the key of the bottomless pit and a great chain in his hand.

2   And he laid hold on the dragon, that old serpent, which is the Devil, and Satan, and bound him a thousand years,

3   And cast him into the bottomless pit, and shut him up, and set a seal upon him, that he should deceive the nations no more, till the thousand years should be fulfilled: and after that he must be loosed a little season.

4   And I saw thrones, and they sat upon them, and judgment was given unto them: and I saw the souls of them that were beheaded for the witness of Jesus, and for the word of God, and which had not worshipped the beast, neither his image, neither had received his mark upon their foreheads, or in their hands; and they lived and reigned with Christ a thousand years.

5   But the rest of the dead lived not again until the thousand years were finished. This is the first resurrection.

6   Blessed and holy is he that hath part in the first resurrection: on such the second death hath no power, but they shall be priests of God and of Christ, and shall reign with him a thousand years.

7   And when the thousand years are expired, Satan shall be loosed out of his prison,

8   And shall go out to deceive the nations which are in the four quarters of the earth, Gog and Magog, to gather them together to battle: the number of whom is as the sand of the sea.

9   And they went up on the breadth of the earth, and compassed the camp of the saints about, and the beloved city: and fire came down from God out of heaven, and devoured them.

10 And the devil that deceived them was cast into the lake of fire and brimstone, where the beast and the false prophet are, and shall be tormented day and night for ever and ever.

THE THOUSAND-YEAR REIGN

Verses 1–2. Jesus had come and ended the battle of Armageddon. The Antichrist and his false prophet were cast into the lake of fire. Satan is now bound in the bottomless pit for one thousand years. This is what is known as the Millennial Reign because Jesus and those in the first resurrection will rule and reign for a thousand years. How wonderful it will be to live in a world in which Jesus reigns, and Satan is bound and can't bother us.

Verse 4. John sees thrones. Remember we saw that overcomers (born-again believers), now in eternal resurrected bodies, will sit on thrones with Jesus. He also sees the souls of those who were beheaded for not taking the mark. These live and reign with Christ for the thousand years. We also discussed that heaven is God's throne and the earth is His footstool.

Verse 5. The rest of the dead stay dead until after the millennium. This is the first resurrection. Notice who are in the first resurrection: Those who are beheaded for not taking the mark of the beast. Some are going to be martyred by the beast. If the rapture is pre-trib, how did the martyrs get resurrected before the Great Tribulation? First would mean there is nothing before. If you are first in a line, there is no one before you. That is what makes you first. I mentioned earlier in this series that there cannot be a bunch of resurrections in the first resurrection.

Verse 6. Those who were raptured and have their resurrected body will not be subject to the Great White Throne Judgment and will not be subject to being cast into the lake of fire, which is the second death, as we will see later in this chapter.

Verses 7–9. Satan is loosed. He goes out to deceive nations all over the earth. Gog and Magog are mentioned. Gog and Magog are discussed in a war in Ezekiel 38. Some have said this war is the battle Armageddon and others feel it is a war that occurs before the Tribulation period. This is the only place Gog and Magog are mentioned in the book of Revelation. I wonder if this war here, after the millennial reign is not the war mentioned in Ezekiel. Much about both wars is similar, such as Israel dwelling in safety (Israel certainly doesn't feel safe now), and in both wars, God destroys with fire from heaven. Satan and his army fight against the saints all over the earth and also come against Jerusalem, the Holy City. Verse 8 says that Satan is able to acquire an army the number as the sand of the sea. I had wondered why Satan was loosed. He was already bound, why let him loose again to cause trouble? Why didn't Jesus just cast him into the lake of fire earlier with the beast and his false prophet? I realized that amazingly, there are many in the land, even after a thousand years, who would still choose Satan over Jesus. God allows people to make the choice of whom they will serve. Those who were in the rapture had already made the choice to serve Jesus.

Verse 10. God ends the battle, and Satan is finally cast into the lake of fire to be tormented day and night forever.

Revelation 20: 11 – 15

11　And I saw a great white throne, and him that sat on it, from whose face the earth and the heaven fled away; and there was found no place for them.

12　And I saw the dead, small and great, stand before God; and the books were opened: and another book was opened, which is the book of life: and the dead were judged out of those things which were written in the books, according to their works.

13　And the sea gave up the dead which were in it; and death and hell delivered up the dead which were in them: and they were judged every man according to their works.

14　And death and hell were cast into the lake of fire. This is the second death.

15　And whosoever was not found written in the book of life was cast into the lake of fire.

THE GREAT WHITE THRONE JUDGMENT

Verse 11. When the Great White Throne Judgment occurs after the thousand-year reign, it says that the earth and heaven fled away from the face of God, and there was found no place for them. In Genesis 1, it says God created the heavens and the earth. This heaven is not referring to the spiritual heaven in which God abides, but the earth's atmosphere and possibly the whole physical realm of the universe including the sun, moon, and stars. God created the whole universe. If it fled away and was not found, did it go into a black hole, or does the universe collapse back to a minute speck?

2 Peter 3: 10 –13

10　But the day of the Lord will come as a thief in the night; in the which the heavens shall pass away with a great noise, and the elements shall melt with fervent heat, the earth also and the works that are therein shall be burned up.

11 Seeing then that all these things shall be dissolved, what manner of persons ought ye to be in all holy conversation and godliness,

12 Looking for and hasting unto the coming of the day of God, wherein the heavens being on fire shall be dissolved, and the elements shall melt with fervent heat?

13 Nevertheless we, according to his promise, look for new heavens and a new earth, wherein dwelleth righteousness.

Second Peter 3:10 says the heavens shall pass away, and the earth will melt with fervent heat. Verse 12 says the heavens would be on fire and be dissolved. Peter then speaks of a new heaven and a new earth. Could it be that the earth catches fire and melts as it falls into the sun? It mentions in verse 10 that the earth would pass away with a great noise. Will the universe end in a great fiery explosion? However it happens, these scriptures are definitely saying the earth will pass away just as Jesus said (Matt. 24:35). Some have said that the earth will always exist, and the "pass away" just means that the earth would be made new. The scripture that has been used in association with that idea is found in Genesis.

Genesis 8: 22

22 While the earth remaineth, seedtime and harvest, and cold and heat, and summer and winter, and day and night shall not cease.

This is not saying that the earth will always remain. It says *as long as the earth remains* there will be seedtime and harvest. This, by the way, negates the climate change doomsayers. There will be a time as it says in Revelation 20 and 1 Peter 3 that the earth will melt and pass away, but it will be after Jesus has returned and reigns for a thousand years. Until that time, we are promised seedtime and harvest and the seasons.

Verse 12. John sees the dead small and great stand before God. Books are opened and the Book of Life. This suggests that there are different books.

Psalms 56: 8

8 Thou tellest my wanderings: put thou my tears into thy bottle: are they not in thy book? Psalms 69: 28 28 Let them be blotted out of the book of the living, and not be written with the righteous.

Psalms 139: 16

16 Thine eyes did see my substance, yet being unperfect; and in thy book all my members were written, which in continuance were fashioned, when as yet there was none of them.

Revelation 13: 8

8 And all that dwell upon the earth shall worship him, whose names are not written in the book of life *of the Lamb* slain from the foundation of the world.

There is more than one book. In the Psalms, David says that all our members (parts of our body) are written in a book. In Ps. 139: 28 he speaks of removing people from the book of the living and not writing them in a book with the righteous. This seems to imply to me that the book of the righteous is a different book. In Rev. 13: 8 it states that only those not written in the Lamb's book of life will take the mark of the beast. It does not say that people's names will be removed after taking the mark. The point I am making, is that I think there is a difference between the book of life in which everyone is written, and the Lamb's book of life in which only those born again (born of the Spirit) will be written. In the letters to the churches Jesus makes reference to repenting lest names be removed from the book of life. Names can be written and they can be removed.

Those whose names are not written in the Lamb's book of life (because they never received Jesus's gift of salvation) will be cast into the lake of fire.

Verses 13–15. (Rev. 20.) John sees the dead. The dead in the sea, and death and hell give up the dead. I realized for the first time on about the forty-eighth round of reading Revelation in a loop that the dead are raised and judged. No "living" are mentioned. John sees only the dead raised and judged at the White Throne Judgment. The world at this time had literally ended. All who were left were the dead. Those who died during the thousand-year reign and those who die when the world comes to an end, God raises to be judged. This group is not those that were caught up in the rapture, the first resurrection. These are the rest of the dead. Those not found in the Book of Life are cast into the lake of fire where Satan, the beast, and the false prophet are. This is the second death. There may be some in this group of raised dead who accepted Christ during the thousand years and are found in the Book of Life.

Revelation 21: 1-5

1   And I saw a new heaven and a new earth: for the first heaven and the first earth were passed away; and there was no more sea.

2   And I John saw the holy city, New Jerusalem, coming down from God out of heaven, prepared as a bride adorned for her husband.

3   And I heard a great voice out of heaven saying, Behold, the tabernacle of God is with men, and he will dwell with them, and they shall be his people, and God himself shall be with them, and be their God.

4   And God shall wipe away all tears from their eyes; and there shall be no more death, neither sorrow, nor crying, neither shall there be any more pain: for the former things are passed away.

5   And he that sat upon the throne said, Behold,
I make all things new. And he said unto me,
Write: for these words are true and faithful.

THE NEW EARTH

Verse 1. John sees a new heaven and a new earth with no sea. If the whole physical universe is gone, this new earth may be an earth in the spiritual realm. No sea could mean no nations or it could mean there will actually be no ocean. The first heaven and earth are passed away.

Verse 2. John sees the New Jerusalem coming down to the new earth prepared as a bride adorned for her husband. This New Jerusalem does not appear until the new earth after the thousand year reign and the final judgment. The rest of the scriptures in this chapter are similar to those that are mentioned after John sees the 144,000 being sealed. (Rev 7).

Verses 3 – 5. God will dwell on the new earth. He will wipe away all tears and there will be no more crying, death or sorrow, or pain. All things are made new.

Revelation 21: 9 -10, 12, 16-17, 19, 21-23

9   And there came unto me one of the seven
angels which had the seven vials full of the
seven last plagues, and talked with me, saying,
Come hither, I will shew thee the bride, the
Lamb's wife.

10 And he carried me away in the spirit to a great
and high mountain, and shewed me that great
city, the holy Jerusalem, descending out of
heaven from God,

12 And had a wall great and high, and had twelve
gates, and at the gates twelve angels, and
names written thereon, which are the names
of the twelve tribes of the children of Israel:

16 And the city lieth foursquare, and the length is
as large as the breadth: and he measured the

city with the reed, twelve thousand furlongs. The length and the breadth and the height of it are equal.

17 And he measured the wall thereof, an hundred and forty and four cubits, according to the measure of a man, that is, of the angel.

19 And the foundations of the wall of the city were garnished with all manner of precious stones.

21 And the twelve gates were twelve pearls; every several gate was of one pearl: and the street of the city was pure gold, as it were transparent glass.

22 And I saw no temple therein: for the Lord God Almighty and the Lamb are the temple of it.

23 And the city had no need of the sun, neither of the moon, to shine in it: for the glory of God did lighten it, and the Lamb is the light thereof.

Verse 9. John is shown the bride, the Lamb's wife. I have always understood that the bride is the church, the body of Christ. Paul mentions a man and wife being one flesh then says he is speaking concerning Christ and the church.

Ephesians 5:31-32

31 For this cause shall a man leave his father and mother, and shall be joined unto his wife, and they two shall be one flesh.

32 This is a great mystery: but I speak concerning Christ and the church.

Verses 10 – 17. He was told he would be shown the bride, and now he sees the New Jerusalem. John then describes the New Jerusalem. Is John seeing a vision that represents the bride, or is this an actual city: Or both? You can read the glorious description of this city. The foundations have the names of the twelve apostles and the church is built on the apostles and prophets. (Eph 2:20) The city has streets of gold. We are tried by fire as pure gold. (I Pe 1:7) The measurements of the city as mentioned previously are four-square, a multiple of 12,000 (12,000 X 12,000. The walls measure 144,000 cubits. Twelve is the number of government. The 144,000 sealed we are told are the redeemed. So much symbolism is here.

Verse 21. There are twelve pearly gates and each gate is one pearl. That is a mighty big oyster. Actually, God can make a large pearl the size of a gate. The gates have the name of the twelve tribes of Israel.

Verse 22. God and the Lamb are the temple. Here are some interesting scriptures:

2 Corinthians 6:16

16 And what agreement hath the temple of God with idols? for *ye are the temple* of the living God; as God hath said, *I will dwell in them*, and *walk in them*; and I will be their God, and they shall be my people.

1 Corinthians 3:16-17

16 Know ye not that *ye are the temple* of God, and that the *Spirit of God dwelleth* in you?

17 If any man defile the temple of God, him shall God destroy; for the temple of God is holy, which temple ye are.

1 Corinthians 6:19

19 What? know ye not that *your body is the temple* of the Holy Ghost which is in you, which ye have of God, and ye are not your own?

Ephesians 2:20-22

20 And are *built upon the foundation of the apostles* and prophets, Jesus Christ himself being the chief corner stone;

21 In whom all the building fitly framed together groweth unto an *holy temple* in the Lord:

22 In whom ye also are builded together for an habitation of through the Spirit.

These scriptures say we (the church, or born-again believers) are the temple in which God dwells. Are these just saying we are to be like a temple or is this how God and the Lamb will dwell in the temple on the new earth? Notice Ephesians 2:20 (as mentioned earlier) speaks of us being built on the foundation of the apostles and the prophets. The twelve foundation stones of the New Jerusalem have the names of the apostles.

Hebrews 12:18, 22 – 23

18 For ye are not come unto the mount that might be touched, and that burned with fire, nor blackness, and darkness, and tempest,

22 But ye are come unto mount Sion, and unto the *city* of the living God, the *heavenly Jerusalem*, and to an innumerable company of angels,

23 To the general assembly and *church* of the firstborn, which are written in heaven, and to God the Judge of all, and to the spirits of just men made perfect,

City, heavenly Jerusalem, church? As mentioned earlier John was told he would be shown the bride, the Lamb's wife and he looked and saw a city. Is this just telling us that we are to be God's temple now, and city now, until He makes the new earth and then will actually dwell with us? I leave the questions with you to enjoy meditating on.

Verse 23. God and Jesus are the light. The city has no need of the sun or moon. It might be a good thing if the sun is passed away and this is a new earth. God's light lights heaven now. (The spiritual realm). If this new earth is in the spiritual realm, and God moves to the earth, God and Jesus will be the source of light.

Daniel 12:2-3

2   And many of them that sleep in the dust of the earth shall awake, some to everlasting life, and some to shame and everlasting contempt.

3   And they that be wise shall as the brightness *shine* of the firmament; and they that turn many to righteousness as the stars for ever and ever.

Matthew 13:40-43

40 As therefore the tares are gathered and burned in the fire; so shall it be in the end of this world.

41 The Son of man shall send forth his angels, and they shall gather out of his kingdom all things that offend, and them which do iniquity;

42 And shall cast them into a furnace of fire: there shall be wailing and gnashing of teeth.

43 *Then shall the righteous shine forth as the sun* in the kingdom of their Father. Who hath ears to hear, let him hear.

Revelation 22: 1 – 5, 11 – 14, 16 – 21

1   And he shewed me a pure river of water of life, clear as crystal, proceeding out of the throne of God and of the Lamb.

2   In the midst of the street of it, and on either side of the river, was there the tree of life, which bare twelve manner of fruits, and yielded her fruit every month: and the leaves of the tree were for the healing of the nations.

3   And there shall be no more curse: but the throne of God and of the Lamb shall be in it; and his servants shall serve him:

4   And they shall see his face; and his name shall be in their foreheads.

5   And there shall be no night there; and they need no candle, neither light of the sun; for the Lord God giveth them light: and they shall reign for ever and ever.

11 He that is unjust, let him be unjust still: and he which is filthy, let him be filthy still: and he that is righteous, let him be righteous still: and he that is holy, let him be holy still.

12 And, behold, I come quickly; and my reward is with me, to give every man according as his work shall be.

13 I am Alpha and Omega, the beginning and the end, the first and the last.

14 Blessed are they that do his commandments, that they may have right to the tree of life, and may enter in through the gates into the city.

16 I Jesus have sent mine angel to testify unto you these things in the churches. I am the root and the offspring of David, and the bright and morning star.

17 And the Spirit and the bride say, Come. And let him that heareth say, Come. And let him that is athirst come. And whosoever will, let him take the water of life freely.

18 For I testify unto every man that heareth the words of the prophecy of this book, If any man shall add unto these things, God shall add unto him the plagues that are written in this book:

19 And if any man shall take away from the words of the book of this prophecy, God shall take away his part out of the book of life, and out of the holy city, and from the things which are written in this book.

20 He which testifieth these things saith, Surely
     I come quickly. Amen. Even so, come, Lord
     Jesus.

21 The grace of our Lord Jesus Christ be with you
     all. Amen.

Verse 1. We see a river of life proceeding out of the throne of God. I discussed previously about a throne being a symbol of God's authority. Are there actual thrones? Some of these questions we may not get answered until we are actually there. There will probably be many things that will surprise us. Just like if a baby in the womb could understand language and you tried to describe what it would be like to be born, there is no way the baby could picture being able to see a wonderful, big world; hearing sharply not muffled; breathing air not liquid and being able to move around freely. One of the things I hope for is that since it is a spiritual earth, there won't be any dust. There may be some who love to dust but I sure don't.

The most glorious thing to me about the new earth will be to live in a place where God and Jesus dwell, everyone there has received Jesus and is living in a resurrected body and there is no satanic influence. Believers are to live in this physical life aware that God dwells in them by His spirit, but we "leak" and have to be continually being filled with His Spirit and walk in the Spirit. Still, we do not have to wait until we go to heaven or until there is a new earth before we can experience God's glorious presence and the peace that Jesus, the Prince of Peace gives us.

Romans 14:17

17 For the kingdom of God is not meat and drink;
     but righteousness, and peace, and joy in the
     Holy Ghost.

Verses 2–5. The tree of life is present with twelve manner of fruit. Is this more symbolism? There is no more curse. There is no night; no sun is needed.

Verses 11–21. Starting with verse 11 John is now through seeing visions and the visions are not being discussed anymore. Jesus tells him He sent His angel to tell him about everything. He says not to add to or take from the prophecy of Revelation. This would be a deliberate adding or taking away. I don't think this means an inadvertent mistake due to not understanding correctly. It would be wise to ensure that our heart and motives are correct when we look into Revelation and try to learn and understand it. Jesus says He comes quickly, and John says, "Even so, come, Lord Jesus."

We are victorious in the end. Satan is gone forever and ever. The battle is won. Because Jesus overcame, we too are overcomers. From Genesis to Revelation we see the plan of God and His purpose for mankind. When Adam sinned, we lost an existence in paradise. Now, paradise has been regained. Had we never known any other existence but one like heaven, we could not have been able to make an informed choice. We would have been like a husband and wife in an arranged marriage. As spirit beings, we had an ability to choose God's love or reject it. God sets before us life and death and wants us to choose life. In Jesus, is life.

Deuteronomy 30:19

19　I call heaven and earth to record this day against you, that I have set before you life and death, blessing and cursing: therefore *choose life*, that both thou and thy seed may live:

John 1:4

4　In him was life; and the life was the light of men.

John 14:6

6　Jesus saith unto him, I am the way, the truth, and the life: no man cometh unto the Father, but by me.

Starting even in this life, we have an eternity to live a glorious existence in the presence of God and Jesus!

REFERENCES

1. **Pastor Dr. Ken Jackson**
   Christian Life Church
   38 Highway 82
   Eufaula, AL 35027
   www.clceufaula.com

2. **LaHaye, T.; Jenkins, B.,** (1995),
   Left Behind,
   Illinois: Tyndale House Publishers, Inc.

3. **Irvin Baxter**
   Endtime Ministries, Inc.
   P.O. Box 940729
   Plano, TX 75094
   End of the Age/TV
   www.endtime.com

4. **Shoebat, W.; Richardson, J.,** (2010),
   God's War on Terror: Islam Prophecy and the Bible,
   Massachusetts: Top Executive Media